Papatango Theatre Company in ~~a~~
the Bush Theatre present

The world premiere of the winner of the
2020 Papatango New Writing Prize

OLD BRIDGE

by Igor Memic

Old Bridge was first produced by Papatango Theatre Company at the
Bush Theatre from 21 October – 20 November 2021.

OLD BRIDGE

by Igor Memic

Cast

Emina	**Susan Lawson-Reynolds**
Mili	**Dino Kelly**
Mina	**Saffron Coomber**
Leila	**Rosie Gray**
Sasha	**Emilio Iannucci**

Director	**Selma Dimitrijevic**
Movement Director	**Georgina Lamb**
Set Designer	**Oli Townsend**
Costume Designer	**Natalie Pryce**
Lighting Designer	**Aideen Malone**
Sound Designer	**Max Pappenheim**
Intimacy Director	**Yarit Dor**
Dramaturg	**George Turvey**
Producer	**Chris Foxon**
Associate Lighting Designer	**Simisola Majekodunmi**
Production Manager	**Tabitha Piggott for eStage**
Stage Manager	**Lois Sime**
Assistant Producer	**Robyn Bennett**
Programmer	**Matthew Carnazza**

The performance lasts approximately 120 minutes including an interval.

Cast and Creative Team

Saffron Coomber | Mina

Saffron trained at RADA. She was nominated for Best West End Debut at The Stage Debut Awards 2019 for her role in *Emilia*. Saffron was the recipient of the Carleton Hobbs Bursary for the BBC in 2018.

Theatre includes: *Leopards* (Rose Theatre), *Emilia* (West End), *Sonnet Sunday* (Shakespeare's Globe) and *A New and Better You* (Yard Theatre).

Film includes: *Viral*, *Electricity*, and *Dustbin Baby*.

Television includes: *The Deceived*, *Strike: Lethal White*, *Small Axe*, *Flack*, *Cuffs*, *EastEnders*, *Youngers*, *Holby City*, *Tracy Beaker: Series 1 – 3*, *Runaway* and *The Bill*.

Radio includes: *Writ in Water*, *Delete*, *The Archers*, *CANE*, *Bird in The Hand* and appearances on *The Radio Drama Company*.

Rosie Gray | Leila

Rosie is a British/Irish actor and theatre-maker and a co-director of Barrel Organ Theatre Company. She trained at Bristol Old Vic Theatre School.

Theatre includes: *Andromeda* (Nottingham Playhouse & CPT), *Anyone's Guess How We Got Here* (Royal Exchange Theatre, Manchester/UK tour), *Julius Caesar* (Bristol Old Vic), *Our Town* (Circomedia), *Some People Talk About Violence* (New Diorama/UK tour) and *Nothing* (Lyric Hammersmith).

Film includes: *Hurricane*, *The Writer's Retreat*, *Redisplacement* and *Lara & Bath Salts*.

Rosie was Assistant Director on Damsel Productions's *Grotty* (Bunker Theatre).

Emilio Iannucci | Sasha

Emilio trained at Royal Central School of Speech and Drama.

Theatre includes: *Around the World in 80 Days*, *Hello and Goodbye* and *The Book of Dragons* (York Theatre Royal), *Romeo and Juliet*, *Richard III*, *Macbeth* and *A Midsummer Night's Dream* (Shakespeare's Rose Theatre), *Peter Pan* (Mercury Theatre), *The Snow Dragon* (Tall Stories/UK tour), and *Twelfth Night* and *Henry V* (Pendley Shakespeare Festival).

Film includes: *Death of Stalin* and *Gloss* (web series).

Television includes: *Traitors*.

Emilio is co-founder of the physical theatre collective Vantage Point who debuted with *This Might Be It* at Theatre N16.

Dino Kelly | Mili

Dino trained at RADA.

Film includes: *The Good Liar, Cliffs of Freedom* and *One Shot*.

Television includes: *Invasion, Peaky Blinders, Inside No.9, Don't Forget the Driver, Pandora, Berlin Station, Silent Witness, Mallorca Files, The Hellenes* and *Heimebane*.

Susan Lawson-Reynolds | Emina

Theatre includes: *Harry Potter and the Cursed Child* (Palace Theatre), *People, Places and Things* (Headlong/National Theatre/UK tour), *Disgraced* (English Theatre Frankfurt), *To Kill a Mockingbird* (Regent's Park Open Air Theatre/UK tour/Barbican), *No Rhyme* (Brockley Jack Studio), *The Scottsboro Boys* (Young Vic), *A Clockwork Orange, Hansel and Gretel, The Snow Queen, Da Boyz, Aeroplane Man* and *Jack and the Beanstalk,* (Theatre Royal Stratford East), *Cat on a Hot Tin Roof* (Novello Theatre), *The Harder They Come* (Playhouse Theatre/Barbican/Theatre Royal Stratford East/Adrienne Arts Centre, Miami/Canon Theatre, Toronto), *Anansi & The Magic Mirror, Anansi Trades Places* and *Ska By Day* (Talawa) and *Grace and the Don* (Arts Theatre).

Film includes: *Why Wouldn't I Be?, Masaryk, London Road* and *White Liar* (short).

Television includes: *Suspicion, The Sandman* and *Michael Jackson: Man In The Mirror.*

Associate Director credits include: *Bubbly Black Girl Sheds Her Chameleon Skin* (Theatre Royal Stratford East).

Choreography credits include: *Ska By Day* (Talawa/Greenwich Theatre).

Susan was Associate Choreographer on *The Wiz* (Birmingham Rep/West Yorkshire Playhouse) and Assistant Choreographer on *The Harder They Come* (Playhouse Theatre London/Theatre Royal Stratford East/Barbican/Adrienne Arts Centre Miami/Canon Theatre Toronto).

Igor Memic | Playwright

Igor is originally from Mostar. He grew up in London after leaving Yugoslavia in 1992 and studied at the University of Liverpool and the Royal Central School of Speech and Drama. *Old Bridge* marks his professional debut.

Selma Dimitrijevic | Director

Selma is a director, writer and dramaturg working in theatre and opera. Her recent work includes the libretto for Olivier Award-nominated *Berenice* at the Royal Opera House, dramaturgy for Sting's musical *The Last Ship* (UK, US and Canadian tour) and writing *Dr Frankenstein*, a new gender-disrupted version of Mary Shelley's novel (UK, US and Canadian tour). In the UK her work has been presented by venues such as Northern Stage, Traverse Theatre, Dundee Rep, Theatre Royal Exchange, Sheffield Theatres, Theatre Royal Bath, Hull Truck, Nuffield Southampton, Curve Leicester, Almeida Theatre and Royal Opera House. Her plays have been translated and performed around the world, including productions in Europe, USA, Canada, India, Australia and Russia. She is Jerwood Artistic Adviser and Unlimited Ally.

Georgina Lamb | Movement Director

Theatre credits include: *Piaf* (Nottingham Playhouse), *Assassins* (also Associate Director, Nottingham Playhouse/Watermill Theatre), *Shadowlands*, *The Midnight Gang*, *A Christmas Carol*, *Grimm Tales* and *The Witches* (Chichester Festival Theatre), *Macbeth* (Chichester Festival Theatre/West End/BAM New York/ Broadway), *Six Characters in Search of an Author* (Chichester Festival Theatre/ Headlong/West End), *Ghost Quartet* (Boulevard Theatre), *Genesis Inc* (Hampstead Theatre), *Frozen* (also Associate Director, West End), *Much Ado About Nothing* (West End), *Chimerica* (Almeida Theatre/West End), *Kiss of the Spider Woman* and *The White Devil* (Menier Chocolate Factory), *A Christmas Carol*, *Titus Andronicus*, *Roaring Girl* and *Romeo and Juliet* (RSC), *Babette's Feast* (Print Room), *Sweeney Todd* (West End/Barrow Street Theatre, New York, Lucille Lortel Award nomination for Outstanding Choreography), *Othello*, *The Comedy of Errors*, *Holy Warriors*, *Doctor Faustus*, *The Frontline*, *Romeo and Juliet*, *A Midsummer Night's Dream*, *The Merchant of Venice*, *The Taming of the Shrew*, *King Lear* and *As You Like It* (Shakespeare's Globe), *Running Wild* and *Macbeth* (Regent's Park Open Air Theatre), *Sleeping Beauty* (Watermill Theatre), *Wit* and *Too Clever By Half* (Royal Exchange Theatre, Manchester), *East is East* and *Precious Little Talent* (Trafalgar Studios), *Every Last Trick*, *The Duchess of Malfi*, *The Talented Mr Ripley*, *The Prime of Miss Jean Brodie* and *The Glass Cage* (Royal & Derngate), *The Ritual Slaughter of Gorge Mastromas* (Royal Court), *Cinderella: The Midnight Princess* and *The Three Musketeers* (Rose Theatre Kingston), *The Lion, the Witch and the Wardrobe* (Kensington Palace Gardens), *Dream Story*, *Electra* and *Lulu* (Gate Theatre), *A Midsummer Night's Dream* and *Paradise Lost* (Headlong), *The Game of Love and Chance* (Salisbury Playhouse), *Gambling* (also co-Director, Soho Theatre), *King Lear* (Headlong/Liverpool Everyman/Young Vic), *Far from the Madding Crowd* (ETT), *The Secret Garden* (Storyhouse Chester), *Never Try This At Home* and *Hopelessly Devoted* (Birmingham Rep) and *The Shops* (Royal Opera House).

Film includes: *Macbeth*.

Television includes *True Stories* (BAFTA nominated), *Once Upon a Time* and *Hansel and Gretel* (BAFTA nominated).

Oli Townsend | Set Designer

Set and costume designs include: *Macbeth* (Royal Exchange Theatre, Manchester), *Così Fan Tutte, Pelleas et Mellisande, Werther* and *The Tales of Hoffmann* (English Touring Opera), *The Caretaker* (Bristol Old Vic), *Grounded, The Christians* and *Wittenberg* (Gate Theatre), *Choir of Man* (world tour), *The Darkest Corners* and *Two Man Show* (RashDash), *We Want You To Watch* (National Theatre/RashDash), *Islands* and *Incognito* (Bush Theatre), *The Art of Dying* (Royal Court), *The Measures Taken* (Alexander Whitley Dance), *L'Elisir D'Amore* and *Rodelinda* (Scottish Opera), *The Gamblers, Dead To Me* and *Gods Are Fallen* and *All Safety Gone* (Greyscale), *The Coronation of Poppea* and *Macbeth* (Blackheath Halls Opera) and *Blood Wedding* (Royal & Derngate). Between 2013–2016, Oli designed the sets for the Lyric Hammersmith's Christmas pantomime.

Costume designs include: *Wozzeck* (English National Opera), *The Lighthouse* (ROH Linbury), *Big Maggie* (Druid) and *In Wonderland*, a film by Iona Firouzabadi.

Oli has also provided art direction for branded content with Jungle Creations & Seldom Differ. In 2018, Oli cycled from Bristol to Bangkok, working on In Tandem Stories in partnership with the non-profit kindness.org. He has written about the experience for *The Guardian, Lonely Planet,* and *WildBounds.*

Natalie Pryce | Costume Designer

Set and costume designs include: *Red Velvet* (RADA), *846 Live* (Theatre Royal Stratford East), *Me For The World* (Young Vic), *Ducklings* (Royal Exchange Theatre, Manchester) and, as co-set and costume designer, *For All the Women Who Thought They Were Mad* (Hackney Showroom) and *Not Now, Bernard* (Unicorn Theatre).

Costume designs include: *White Noise* (Bridge Theatre), *Is God Is* (Royal Court), *Anna X* (West End), *Tales of the Turntable* (Zoonation) and, as costume supervisor, *The Winter's Tale* (Shakespeare's Globe).

Film includes: *Good Grief, Fourteen Fractures, Myrtle, Fellow Creatures, Swept Under Rug* and (as costume trainee) *My Name is Leon.*

Aideen Malone | Lighting Designer

Previous credits at the Bush Theatre include: *Dogs Barking, Hijra* and *Flamingos.*

Other theatre credits include: *Carousel* (Regent's Park Open Air Theatre), *Hamlet* (Young Vic), *A Kind of People* (Royal Court), *Death of a Salesman* (Young Vic & Piccadilly), *A Monster Calls* (Old Vic/Bristol Old Vic), *Worst Witch* (Vaudeville), *Brighton Rock* and *A View from a Bridge* (York Theatre Royal), *La Strada* (The Other Palace), *Jane Eyre* and *Peter Pan* (National Theatre/Bristol Old Vic), *Fiddler on the Roof* and *Conquest to the North Pole* (Liverpool Everyman), *Hetty Feather* (Duke of York's Theatre), *Frankenstein* (Living Spit), *Napoleon Disrobed* and *The Strange Tale of Stan Laurel and Charlie Chaplin* (Told By An Idiot) and *A Raisin in the Sun* and *Talent* (Sheffield Theatres).

Dance credits include: *Outwitting The Devil* and *Kaash* (Akram Kahn Co), *Darbar Festival* (Sadler's Wells), *Raft* (GED), *Unkindest Cut* (Sadhana), *Time Over Distance Over Time* (Liz Roche) and *La Tete* (Jasmin Vardimon).

Opera credits include: *Ariodante, The Turn of the Screw, The Marriage of Figaro, A Midsummer Night's Dream, Mary Queen of Scots, Così Fan Tutte, Jenufa* and *Tosca* (English Touring Opera).

Max Pappenheim | Sound Designer

Theatre credits include: *Cruise, The Night of the Iguana* and *Cookies* (West End), *Assembly* and *The Way of the World* (Donmar Warehouse), *The Children* (Royal Court/Broadway), *Looking Good Dead* (UK tour/Peter James Productions), *Macbeth* (Chichester Festival Theatre), *Malindadzimu, Dry Powder, Sex with Strangers* and *Labyrinth* (Hampstead Theatre), *Ophelias Zimmer* (Schaubühne, Berlin/Royal Court), *Crooked Dances* (Royal Shakespeare Company), *One Night in Miami* (Nottingham Playhouse), *Waiting for Godot* (Sheffield Crucible), *The Ridiculous Darkness* (Gate Theatre), *Amsterdam, Humble Boy, Blue/Heart* and *The Distance* (Orange Tree Theatre), *The Gaul* (Hull Truck), *Jane Wenham* (Out Of Joint), *My Cousin Rachel, The Habit of Art, Monogamy, Teddy, Toast, Fabric* and *Invincible* (national tours).

Online work includes: *Barnes' People* and *The Haunting of Alice Bowles* (Original Theatre) and *15 Heroines* (Digital Theatre).

Opera includes *Miranda* (Opéra Comique, Pari), *Scraww* (Trebah Gardens), *Vixen* (Vaults/international tour) and *Carmen: Remastered* (Royal Opera House/Barbican).

Radio includes *Home Front*.

Max is Associate Artist of The Faction and Silent Opera.

Yarit Dor | Intimacy Director

Previous credits at the Bush Theatre include *Strange Fruit*.

Theatre credits include: *Rockets and Blue Lights* (National Theatre), *NW Trilogy* (Kiln Theatre), *Changing Destiny* (Young Vic), *Statements After an Arrest Under the Immorality Act* and *Last Easter* (Orange Tree Theatre), *Death of a Salesman* (West End/Young Vic), *Miss Julie* (Storyhouse Chester), *Richard II, Hamlet, As You Like It* and *Much Ado About Nothing* (Shakespeare's Globe), *Daddy* (Almeida Theatre), *Wild East* (Young Vic), *Macbeth* (Royal Exchange Theatre, Manchester), *Assata Taught Me* (Gate Theatre), *The Effect* (Boulevard Theatre), *Romeo and Juliet, As You Like It* and *A Midsummer Night's Dream* (Shakespeare In The Squares), *Little Voice* and *Disgraced* (Park Theatre) and *Titus Andronicus* (Greenwich Theatre).

Dance includes: *Rooms* (Rambert) and *Between A Self And An Other, Leah, 2B* and *Sunday Morning* (Hagit Yakira Company).

Film includes: *The Colour Room*.

Television includes: *The Wheel Of Time, Adult Material, Close To Me, Atlanta, Superhoe, The Girlfriend Experience 3, Spanish Princess 2, Becoming Elizabeth, Domina, White Lines* and *Starstruck*.

George Turvey | Dramaturg

George co-founded Papatango in 2007 and became its sole Artistic Director in January 2013. As a dramaturg, he has led the development of all of Papatango's productions.

Credits as director include: *The Silence and The Noise* (Papatango New Writing Prize 2021, UK tour), *Shook* (Papatango New Writing Prize 2019, Southwark Playhouse/ UK tour, nominated for 7 OffWestEnd Awards and *The Stage* Debut Award for Best Writer; also broadcast on Sky Arts), *Hanna* (Papatango, UK tour), *The Annihilation of Jessie Leadbeater* (Papatango at ALRA), *After Independence* (Papatango at Arcola Theatre, 2016 Alfred Fagon Audience Award, and BBC Radio 4), *Leopoldville* (Papatango at Tristan Bates Theatre) and *Angel* (Papatango at Pleasance London and Tristan Bates Theatre).

George trained as an actor at the Academy of Live and Recorded Arts (ALRA) and has appeared on stage and screen throughout the UK and internationally, including the lead roles in the world première of Arthur Miller's *No Villain* (Old Red Lion Theatre and Trafalgar Studios) and *Batman Live* World Arena Tour.

He is the co-author of *Being A Playwright: A Career Guide for Writers*.

Chris Foxon | Producer

Chris is Executive Director of Papatango.

Theatre credits with the company include: *Some Of Us Exist In The Future*, *The Silence and The Noise* and *Ghost Stories From An Old Country* (Papatango New Writing Prize 2021, UK tour), *Shook* (Papatango New Writing Prize 2019, Southwark Playhouse/UK tour, nominated for 7 OffWestEnd Awards and *The Stage* Debut Award for Best Writer; also broadcast on Sky Arts), *The Funeral Director* (Papatango New Writing Prize 2018, Southwark Playhouse/UK tour), *Hanna* (Arcola Theatre/UK tour), *Trestle* (Papatango New Writing Prize 2017, Southwark Playhouse), *Orca* (Papatango New Writing Prize 2016, Southwark Playhouse), *After Independence* (Arcola Theatre, 2016 Alfred Fagon Audience Award; BBC Radio 4), *Tomcat* (Papatango New Writing Prize 2015, Southwark Playhouse), *Coolatully* (Papatango New Writing Prize 2014, Finborough Theatre), *Unscorched* (Papatango New Writing Prize 2013, Finborough Theatre), and *Pack* and *Everyday Maps for Everyday Use* (Papatango New Writing Prize 2012, Finborough Theatre).

Other theatre credits include *The Transatlantic Commissions* (Old Vic Theatre), *Donkey Heart* (Old Red Lion Theatre/West End), *The Fear of Breathing* (Finborough Theatre/Akasaka Red Theatre, Tokyo), *The Keepers of Infinite Space* (Park Theatre) and *Happy New* (West End).

Chris is the co-author of *Being A Playwright: A Career Guide for Writers*.

Simisola Majekodunmi | Associate Lighting Designer

Simi trained at RADA. Theatre includes *Lucid* and *Tiger Under The Skin* (New Public Company), *Driving Miss Daisy* (York Theatre Royal), *Invisible Harmony* (Southbank Centre), *Seeds* (Tiata Fahodzi/Leeds Playhouse), *Just Another Day and Night* (The Place Theatre), *Living Newspaper Edition 6* and *Is God Is* (Royal Court Theatre), *J'ouvert* (Harold Pinter Theatre) and *Sessions* (Soho Theatre). Theatre as an associate includes *Shoe Lady* (Royal Court Theatre), *15 Heroines* (Jermyn Street Theatre), *Herding Cats* (Soho Theatre) and *The Shark Is Broken* (Ambassadors Theatre).

Robyn Bennett | Assistant Producer

Producing credits include: *Please, Feel Free to Share*, *Years of Sunlight*, *Screens* and *The State We're In* (Theatre503), *Lippy* (Brighton Fringe/Wandsworth Fringe), *nest* (VAULT Festival), *Dr Angelus* (Finborough Theatre) and *Your Ever Loving* (TheatreN16). She is currently the Assistant Producer at Papatango and the Assistant General Manager at Kiln Theatre, and was previously Production Assistant and Executive Assistant at The Old Vic working across productions including *All My Sons*, *A Very Expensive Poison* and *Wise Children*. She has been an Assistant Producer at Watford Palace Theatre, Tara Finney Productions, National Youth Music Theatre and Theatre503, and is Associate Producer at Small Truth Theatre and Scatterjam. www.robynbennett.co.uk

Matthew Carnazza | Programmer

Matthew trained at Rose Bruford College. Theatre credits as lighting designer include: *The Collective* (Dance City Newcastle/UK tour), *Light Shining in Buckinghamshire* (YATI), *Syndrome* (Tristan Bates Theatre), *Vernon God Little* (Stratford Circus), *Our House* and *Bye Bye Birdie* (Italia Conti), *Tutu Trouble* (Fairfields Halls), *JV2 2019* (Sadler's Wells/UK tour), *Duchess of Malfi* (Rose Theatre), *Angry Brigade* (ALRA London), *Limbo* (Summerhall), *Chicago* (Bridewell Theatre), *Also in Watermelon Sugar* (Stanley Halls), *Boys Cry* (Hammersmith Studios) and *The Wedding Singer* (POSK). Theatre credits as associate lighting designer and programmer include: *This is my Room* (Rose Lipman Studio), *Infinite Ways Home* (UK tour), *Mikado* (UK tour), *Bright Lights Big City* (Italia Conti), *Version 2.0* (Leicester Square Theatre), *Angry Brigade* (ALRA London), *Zemsta* (POSK), *The Mysteries* (YATI) and *In the Heights* (Bridewell Theatre). Film credits as lighting director include: *Wait For Me* and *POSK Online*.

Production Acknowledgements

2020 Papatango New Writing Prize Reading Team | **Olu Alakija, Lucy Allan, Ayad Andrews, Safaa Bensom-Effiom, Jo Bowman, Kate Brower, Michael Byrne, Bridie Donaghy, Antonia Georgieva, Karis Halsall, Richard Hammarton, Rebecca Hill, Naomi Joseph, Jonny Kelly, Shabnom Khanom, Lily Levinson, Emily Lunnon, Gemma Murray, Louis Shankar, Blythe Stewart, Krystal Sweedman, Roisin Symes, Emma Wilkinson and Matt Woodhead**

Rehearsal Photography | **The Other Richard**

Production Photography | **Marc Brenner**

Press Representation | **Kate Morley PR**

R&D Cast | **Alex Austin**, **Saffron Coomber**, **Thea Mayeux**, **Clare Perkins** and **Max Runham**

Many thanks to the 2020 Papatango New Writing Prize's generous supporters: Arts Council England; Backstage Trust; Boris Karloff Charitable Foundation; Cockayne – Grants for the Arts and The London Community Foundation; Foyle Foundation; Golsoncott Foundation; Harold Hyam Wingate Foundation; the Royal Victoria Hall Foundation; and the Garfield Weston Foundation.

With Special Thanks | **Ambersphere Solutions**

PAPA tango

'Remarkable unearthers of new talent' *Evening Standard*

Papatango was founded to champion the best new playwriting talent in the UK and Ireland. We discover and launch playwrights through free, open application opportunities. Our motto is simple: all you need is a story.

Our flagship programme is the Papatango New Writing Prize, the UK's first and still only annual award to guarantee a playwright a full production, publication, royalties and an unprecedented commission for a second play. Prize-winners have transferred worldwide, received many awards, and risen to the forefront of theatre, film and TV.

The Prize is free to enter and assessed anonymously. All entrants receive feedback on their scripts, an unmatched commitment to supporting playwrights. 1,504 entries were received in 2020, meaning the Prize continues to receive more annual submissions than any other UK playwriting award – and yet is unique in giving support to all.

Papatango also run an annual Resident Playwright scheme, taking an emerging playwright through commissioning, development and production. It gives in-depth, sustained support to writers who might not otherwise be in a position to win the Prize, for lack of access to resources such as training, commissions or mentoring. Our Residents have toured the UK, adapted their work for radio, and transitioned to full-time careers as writers.

We use the astonishing success of the writers discovered and launched through these opportunities to inspire others that they too can make and enjoy top-class theatre. Our GoWrite programme delivers extensive, free playwriting opportunities nationwide. Young people in state schools write plays which are professionally performed and published, while adults join workshops, complete six-month courses at a variety of regional venues culminating in free public performances, or access fortnightly one-to-one career advice sessions. GoWrite delivers face-to-face training for over 3000 writers each year, with travel bursaries to enable anyone to access its free opportunities.

Writers launched by Papatango have won BAFTAs, The Times Breakthrough, OffWestEnd, RNT Foundation Playwright and Alfred Fagon Awards, been nominated for the Susan Smith Blackburn Prize and Evening Standard Most Promising Playwright Award, and premiered worldwide.

Our first book *Being A Playwright: A Career Guide for Writers* was published in 2018 ('a phenomenon for playwriting good... a bible for playwrights', Steve Waters).

Online
For up-to-date news and opportunities please visit:

www.facebook.com/pages/PapaTango-Theatre-Company/257825071298

www.twitter.com/PapaTangoTC

www.instagram.com/papatangotc/

www.papatango.co.uk

Bush Theatre

THANK YOU

The Bush Theatre would like to thank all its supporters whose valuable contributions have helped us to create a platform for our future and to promote the highest quality new writing, develop the next generation of creative talent, lead innovative community engagement work and champion diversity.

MAJOR DONORS
Gianni & Michael Alen-Buckley
Charles Holloway
Georgia Oetker
Tim & Cathy Score
Jack Thorne

LONE STARS
Gianni Alen-Buckley
Michael Alen-Buckley
Jacqui Bull
Rafael & Anne-Helene Biosse Duplan
Charles Holloway
Priscilla John
Rosemary Morgan
Georgia Oetker
Susie Simkins

HANDFUL OF STARS
Charlie Bigham
Judy Bollinger
Clyde Cooper
Sue Fletcher
Joanna Kennedy
Simon & Katherine Johnson
Garry Lawrence
V&F Lukey
Anthony Marraccino
Aditya Mittal
Robert Ledger & Sally Moulsdale
Clare Rich
Kit and Anthony Van Tulleken

RISING STARS
David Brooks
Catharine Browne
Matthew Byam Shaw
Philip Cameron & Richard Smith
Esperanza Cerdan
Grace Chan
Lauren Clancy
Tim & Andrea Clark
Sarah Clarke
Susie Cuff
Matthew Cushen
Philippa Dolphin
Jack Gordon & Kate Lacy
Hugh & Sarah Grootenhuis
Thea Guest
Lesley Hill & Russ Shaw
Fiona l'Anson
Davina & Malcolm Judelson
Lynette Linton
Miggy Littlejohns
Judith Mellor
Caro Millington
Danny Morrison
Dan & Laurie Mucha
Rajiv Parkash
Mark & Anne Paterson
Brian Smith
Joe Tinston & Amelia Knott
Peter Tausig
Jan Topham
Guy Vincent & Sarah Mitchell

CORPORATE SPONSORS
Biznography
Dorsett Shepherds Bush
Jamie Lloyd Company
Studio Doug
U+I
Wychwood Media

TRUSTS AND FOUNDATIONS
29th May 1961 Charitable Trust
Christina Smith Foundation
Cockayne Foundation - Grants for the Arts
The Daisy Trust
Esmee Fairbairn
Foyle Foundation
Garfield Weston Foundation
Hammersmith United Charities
The Harold Hyam Wingate Foundation
John Lyon's Charity
Leche Trust
The Martin Bowley Charitable Trust
One anonymous donor
Orange Tree Trust
Royal Victoria Hall Foundation
The Teale Charitable Trust
Tesco Bags of Help
Tudor Trust
Victoria Wood Foundation

bushtheatre.co.uk

Supported by ARTS COUNCIL ENGLAND

If you are interested in finding out how to be involved, please visit **bushtheatre.co.uk/support-us** or email **eleanortindall@bushtheatre.co.uk** or call **020 8743 3584.**

OLD BRIDGE

Igor Memic

With thanks to

George Turvey and Chris Foxon for your unwavering faith in this story. You made a dream come true.

Deirdre O'Halloran and everyone at the Bush. There is love and radiance in that building and it shines from each of you.

Saffron, Dino, Emilio, Rosie, and Susan. Thank you for your bravery, your generosity and your kindness. Two days in and you felt like family.

Adam, Adrian, Cat, Claudia, Edmir, Hannah, Kati and Tim. My guiding lights. I would be lost without you.

To Selma Dimitrijevic, Lois Sime, and every artist who helped make this dream a reality.

To Daisy, I simply wouldn't have made it through this without you.

To Teo, you're more than 'like a brother to me.' You are a brother to me.

To Joanna, for making lockdown unforgettable.

To Jadran, for counting the steps.

To Selma and Almir for your endless love and support.

To Leo, for helping me see the future.

And lastly…

This play is dedicated to my mum and to my grandmother.
These were your stories. All I did was listen x

4

Characters

EMINA, *fifty*
MINA, *from eighteen*
MILI, *from twenty*
LEILA, *from eighteen*
SASHA, *from twenty*

Notes on Performance

Old Bridge is set across two interweaving and overlapping timelines: the past, and the present. Both are designed to flow seamlessly in and out of one another as one fluid narrative.

Notes on the Text

Dialogue written [in square brackets] is spoken by the characters but not heard by the audience.

A dash (–) at the end of a line is interrupted by the next.

Accents and Pronunciation

Mostar, our characters' home town, has a short 'o'. The first syllable rhymes with *cost*, not with *coast*.

Depictions of prayer in Arabic are written phonetically.

The rest will be guided through where necessary.

The characters' accents should reflect the place where this play is being performed. Any words or phrases written in a London dialect can be changed to accommodate this.

This text went to press before the end of rehearsals and so may differ slightly from the play as performed.

PART ONE – Girls Just Want to Have Fun

1.1

Darkness.

From the minaret of a nearby mosque, the Adhan is heard. As the muezzin calls Muslims to prayer, his voice is joined by the ringing of church bells.

They sound in perfect harmony.

Enter EMINA *(fifty), wearing a headscarf.*

She opens the curtains. Daylight illuminates the modest living room and kitchenette of a small flat adorned in traditional Bosnian decor: one part Ottoman, one part Austro-Hungarian, and one part Mediterranean.

On the stove sits a copper džezva [jez-va] *in which her coffee gently cooks. She approaches it and peers inside, stirring its contents patiently. When it's ready, she turns off the heat and places it on a beautifully embossed copper tray. The care and ritual with which she prepares it suggests a lifetime's tradition.*

She sits at the table and pours herself a cup. The smell of fresh coffee and warm copper enriches the air. It overwhelms you.

EMINA. She looks as though she were built by Nature, not by men.

As though Nature herself laid her eyes upon the two halves of this town, carved apart by the very river she placed here millennia ago, and knew at once that these two lands should be united once again… so she grew a bridge. A bridge of stone and vine and iron, which sprouted from the cliffs like the roots of a great tree. Reaching out towards each other slowly, over centuries, until those hands were locked together in an everlasting grip.

Farmers, merchants, kings and emperors, master stonemasons from Rome, Dalmatia and Athens – people came from every corner of the land to cast their eyes on what they thought could never be possible: a bridge of stone across the river Neretva. Each stood dumbstruck by her grandeur, for to see her was to know beyond a shadow of a doubt that men could not have built such a thing, this... colossus of stone, stretching out into the sky; slender and elegant, yet as firm and everlasting as the mountains around her.

And even though she was the only bridge in town, the only bridge for a hundred miles, the name they gave her... was Old Bridge. Because they knew that she had been here precisely since forever, and would be here, still, until the end of time.

Old Bridge... *Stari Most*... Mostar was born that day. And with it a thousand poems, paintings, novels, countless love songs, first dates, first kisses. There's not a story told here that doesn't start with the words 'by Old Bridge' or 'near Old Bridge' or 'you'll never guess who I saw on Old Bridge today.'

And I guess this story isn't any different.

It was the day before the jump. We knew some of the boys would be on the waterfront practising and that's exactly where we were headed. Tourists cling to her railings as they try to cross, staring down at the gaps and imperfections of ancient hands as me and Leila just glide across in heels, making it look easy. Like running up the stairs of your own home; you don't have to look.

Through the market, down the cobble steps, all the way to the river. We take a seat near the water's edge; find that perfect spot where Old Bridge blocks the sun. That summertime buzz of a hundred clamouring voices fills the air until...

Silence. Everyone stops... Everyone looks up.

On her summit stands a silhouette in cruciform. Head up, chest out, arms wide: *Lasta*, we call it... the technique they've used for centuries. All eyes are fixed on him. Not a whisper as he waits... breathes in slowly...

He leans his body forward, flicks his toes, throws his arms out to the side and flies, tearing the clear blue sky in half.

Her eyes follow him as he falls: Five... Four... Three... Two... One...

Not a splash... The most perfect Lasta I had ever seen.

But no one claps. Not yet. It's not the jump that kills you it's the river. It looks tame on the surface but the undercurrent's vicious: if it grabs you by the ankle and you weren't raised on this river then your body's getting washed up on the coast somewhere. We've seen it happen.

Silence... He should be up by now.

A group of tourists smile in ignorant anticipation but the locals just stay quiet. If the silence was uncomfortable before, it's painful now. I'm holding my breath. This boy's either dead or has lungs like a dolphin. And just as Leila grabs my arm and starts to squeeze... a head emerges. I breathe out.

The tourists start clapping but the locals just roll their eyes. The boy looks around expecting a fanfare but there isn't one. Just Leila, cupping her hands around her mouth: 'You swim like you were taught in a bathtub!' Everyone looks over as we burst out laughing. He looks over too. Starts swimming right towards us and we're screaming now, dying of laughter but the more we try to stop the more we can't!

He gets to the riverbank... Every muscle in his body tenses as he pulls himself out of the water, and those smiles get wiped right off our faces.

She walk over to the stereo and presses play. 'Girls Just Want to Have Fun' by Cyndi Lauper blares out loud and fabulous as the apartment disappears, and we're transported to:

1.2

Waterfront, 1988.

MINA *and* LEILA (*both eighteen*) *are sat on the riverbank.*
MINA *wears a bright white dress.*

MILI (*twenty*) *is stood in front of them. Swimming trunks. Wet.*

The music stops abruptly.

MILI. Well? What do you think?

MINA. Excuse me?

MILI. …My jump. What do you think?

MINA. Oh… it was alright I guess. Wasn't really paying
attention.

MILI. What's your name?

MINA. …Mina. This is my friend Leila.

MILI. Hey. That's quite a voice you've got.

LEILA. Oh… that wasn't… no, they were… those guys left.

Silence.

MILI (*to* MINA). I like your dress.

MINA. Thanks, it's Italian.

LEILA. Yeah my mum made it for her.

MINA *stares at her, unimpressed.*

MINA. …So it was like in this copy of *Vogue* my auntie sent
from England… and she made it like *exactly* the same so it's
still… you know it's still… *Italian.*

Silence.

LEILA. Where are you from?

MILI. How do you know I'm not from here?

LEILA. Because you can't swim.

Giggling.

MILI.…Dubrovnik.

MINA. Oh yeah? And what's a Dalmatian boy doing in Mostar?

MILI. Enjoying the view. You watching the jump tomorrow?

MINA. Maybe… Haven't decided yet.

MILI. Cool well, I'm third to jump, so…

LEILA. You're jumping tomorrow?

MILI.…That a problem?

MINA. Depends. You gonna jump like that again?

Giggling.

MILI. I thought you weren't paying attention…

MINA. I wasn't.

MILI. My mistake.

LEILA. It's gonna be windy tomorrow; you sure you know what you're doing?

MILI. A little breeze never hurt anyone.

MINA. You haven't been here long at all, have you?

MILI. Long enough.

MINA. I guess we'll find out tomorrow.

MILI. I guess we will…

MINA. If we can make it.

MILI. Well… maybe I'll see you tomorrow.

MINA. Maybe you will.

Silence.

Exit MILI.

The girls exhale as though they've been holding their breath.

LEILA. Oh. My. God!

MILI (*off*). Mina?

The girls retake their not-so-demure pose.

Enter MILI, *towel in hand, drying his hair.*

MINA....Yes?

MILI. If I win tomorrow, will you marry me?

The girls burst out laughing.

Silence.

Well?

MINA....If you survive tomorrow I'll let you buy me a coffee.

MILI. Deal.

Exit MILI.

1.3

Apartment, present.

EMINA *sits, drinking her coffee.*

EMINA. The day of the jump.

If this were any other day I could tell you exactly who, from my street to the riverbank, would be sat where and doing what; you could set your watch by them. But not today. Today the streets are empty and that suits me just fine; I'm running late, and this is the one and only day in the entire year that my neighbour Mrs Hasanović won't talk at me for twenty minutes and insist I stop for lunch.

I get to Leila's block, heels in hand and out of breath. Find her sat round the back between two buckled railings in the fence, eyebrow raised, staring at her watch; she gave up telling me off a long time ago.

The whole of the waterfront had been cordoned off, and if you weren't there queuing from the break of dawn then love nor money wouldn't get you through... But you don't grow up in a town like this without learning one or two little secrets.

She stubs her cigarette out. Ties her hair back as we climb through the fence. Feet sideways down the gorge, shoes in one hand, clutch bags in the other.

Stone Plateau, 1988.

SASHA (*twenty*) *waits impatiently. A pack of beer bottles under his arm.*

SASHA. Alright, dickheads. What took you so long?

Enter MINA *and* LEILA.

MINA. Sorry, Leila took about ten hours to get ready.

LEILA. ME?! Are you actually serious?

SASHA. Yeah okay, Mina, if that's true then how come she still looks like shit?

LEILA....I will push you and make it look like an accident.

SASHA. I'm joking. You look fine.

LEILA. Fine? I look *fine*? Are you serious? Oh my God thank you so much.

She takes a beer from under his arm and holds the neck out. SASHA *opens it.*

SASHA. Drink fast, you're prickly when you're sober.

LEILA. I'm gonna do it. I'm actually gonna kill him.

Beneath them a crowd of ten thousand spectators goes wild.

SASHA. Can't hear, it's too loud! Was that 'thanks for sorting the beer, Sasha'?

MINA. Guys, they're starting.

LEILA. I said they'll never find your body!

SASHA. You're welcome, any time!

MINA. Guys!

They take a seat on the plateau's edge.

EMINA. On the beaches beneath us, all life is here: ten thousand smiling faces packed on to the waterfront.

Every single resident of Mostar, gathered as they have done on this same day, at this same place, for centuries. And from this little corner of the world, we've got the best view in town.

Twelve young men line up along her thirty-metre arch and wave down towards the crowds as the speakers boom, announcing the start of this year's competition. 'First to jump: Adnan Selimović! Twenty-one, from Luka, Mostar!'

The crowd erupts. It sounds like a football match.

LEILA. Eugh. He's so gross.

SASHA. What do you mean gross, I thought you guys dated?

LEILA....I said he was gross, I didn't say he was ugly.

Wind blows violently. The kids shuffle back from the canyon's edge.

EMINA. Flags and banners pull violently against their masts but he doesn't even flinch. A hundred words for wind... we call this one *Bura*: 'mountain storm'.

He takes his place on the ancient stone, raises up his arms and the crowd falls still. Ten thousand pairs of eyes stare silently at him as he watches the wind. Arms wide, chest out, eyes closed. Feels the gaze of his ancestors as they breathe down his neck...

They whisper to him... *now*.

In unison they watch him fall: Five... Four... Three... Two... One...

Not a splash. Not a sound. Head emerging just as quickly as it entered. He punches the air in triumph as the judges raise their cards to an almost perfect score.

The waterfront erupts.

SASHA. I think his swimming trunks just got even tighter.

EMINA. 'Alexander Bevanda! Twenty-two, from Balnovac, Mostar!'

The crowd cheers.

MINA. Alexi? No, he can't swim *and* think at the same time.

EMINA. He climbs through and curls his toes over the stone; waving down to his friends as he takes his form. Silence as every muscle in his body tenses, holding firm against the wind; reading it like it's a second language.

And when that clear blue sky holds still...

They watch him. Five... Four... Three... Two... One...

They all wince.

Water shoots up into the air, rains down on him as his head emerges; he didn't point his feet in time. The judges confer, raising their cards with fives and sixes.

LEILA. That's too many numbers for him, he probably thinks he's smashed it.

EMINA. Then as he swims back to the riverbank, I feel Leila grab my wrist –

LEILA. There he is!

SASHA. Who?

LEILA. Mina's new lover boy.

MINA. Shut up no he's not.

LEILA. Wipe this bit, babe, you're drooling again.

SASHA. Who is he?

LEILA. Just moved here from the coast.

SASHA. What? You joking? What's he doing up there?

EMINA. 'Next up... Iliya Angelić! Twenty, from... Dubrovnik.'

An instant and deafening silence.

Not a sound... Just the creak of the iron railings as Mili climbs between them. You could hear a toothpick snap. Leila's grip tightens. He lifts his arms up to the side and takes his form; still nothing from the crowd. Just the rumble of the wind as it barges into him. He trembles, grabs the railing.

SASHA. Your boyfriend's gonna get himself killed.

EMINA. Sasha's face straight. Not laughing any more.

MINA. He can jump... I've seen him.

EMINA. But the fear kicks in. The scale of his stupidity hits him hard across the face and you could see it in his eyes a mile away. He doesn't know this town. He doesn't know this river. You jumped off a few cliffs in Croatia, good for you; well now you're gonna get yourself killed. He turns around. The stone steps are calling out to him. Tempting him back down and I can't watch it any more.

I close my eyes and I pray for it to end...

SASHA. Hey, Mina, hold my beer.

MINA.... What? Why?

SASHA *stands up.*

SASHA. COME ON, ILIYAAAA! WOOOOO! YEAH YOU GOT THIS!

MINA. SASHA! What are you doing!

He cups his hands around his mouth, laughing.

SASHA. IL-I-YA! IL-I-YA! IL-I-YA!

EMINA. Ten thousand pairs of eyes have turned towards us as I feel my heart go cold. I bury my face in my hands, begging for the ground to open up and swallow me, but before my prayers are answered.

LEILA. Come on, Iliyaaaa!

MINA. Oh my God, Leila, sit down!

EMINA. She's laughing now as well, offers me her hand but before I can say no...

SASHA *puts his arms under* MINA*'s shoulders and lifts her to her feet.*

I look down at the sea of staring faces and my body freezes. I have to do something... but all I can muster is a slow and steady clap...

MINA *does so.*

And as I stand there clapping like an idiot, a pair of hands beneath joins in.

…Then another.

…Then ten others.

LEILA *and* SASHA *join in.*

Then a hundred more join in, all clapping in a slow and steady rhythm. It gets faster.

Another hundred. Faster.

Then a thousand.

Then ten thousand… clapping faster and faster until the rhythm breaks and the whole of the waterfront erupts into all-out applause. Chills run down my back. I can't believe what I'm seeing. All of Mostar, clapping, cheering for him like he's one of their own.

I look back at Mili, and even though he's miles away I see him smiling. See him looking back at me, and when he does… it feels like time stands still… and we're the only two people on this earth.

Time stops.

I lean forward… and I whisper to him… softly… quietly…

MINA.…Don't fuck this up.

EMINA. And I know that he can hear me.

Time starts again.

Like a conductor before an orchestra, he raises up his arms and the crowd falls still; silence again, the way it should have been. He tenses up his muscles, fights against the mountain wind and it doesn't even flick a hair off his chest.

Now all he has to do is wait.

Hold steady.

Read the wind.

And wait for that perfect –

MINA. WHAT'S HE DOING?!

SASHA drags MINA and LEILA to the ground as a gust nearly flings them from the canyon.

They launch back up and watch in horror: Five... Four... Three... Two...

On 'One' EMINA does a single, loud, echoing clap and everyone but her disappears.

Silence... A long. Painful. Silence.

1.4

Apartment, present.

EMINA *fills a small bowl of water for Wudu: the cleansing ritual done by Muslims before prayer. As she tells her story, she runs water over her arms, face, head, legs and feet.*

EMINA. I can't remember who won that year but Mostar was on fire. Every bar, café, and club was packed so tight that everyone just spilled out onto the streets. Songs and chants that once were unified were now just slurred and rambling noises. And every time the victor was paraded past, carried on the shoulders of his drunken entourage, the crowds would cheer, raise their glasses into the air and rain beer down all over the outfit you've been planning for months.

And when bumping into uncles and exes got too tiresome, we'd make our way down to the riverbank as we always did; a place to smoke away from prying eyes. One of us would always have a pack. Sasha this time. 57s he used to smoke. Slovenian. Cheap as a loaf of bread. They used to pack them upside down so when farmers and factory workers pulled one out of the box they wouldn't get dirt on the bit you put in your mouth.

We take the stone steps down to the waterfront where hours earlier thousands had amassed and now... Not a soul.

Well... Almost.

The Adhan is heard.

A silhouette by the water blocks the moonlight's reflection; a set of shoulders I'd recognise anywhere... Sasha stops dead in his tracks.

His eyes light up with mischief as mine and Leila's hearts sink. 'Sasha,' I tell him... 'don't even think about it!'

The melisma of the muezzin's voice blends into the shredding of an electric guitar: the opening guitar solo of 'When Doves Cry' by Prince.

But before the words have barely left my mouth he's off, and Leila's chasing him!

LEILA (*off*). SASHA! SASHAAA!

The Adhan fades as EMINA *and the apartment disappear.*

Waterfront, 1988.

Moonlight illuminates the river mist.

The music fades into the distant sound of a far-off party.

MILI *sits alone.*

SASHA (*off*). IL-I-YA!... IL-I-YA!... IL-I-YA!

MILI *turns around, startled.*

Enter SASHA, *wearing a 'Choose Life' T-shirt tucked into 501s.*

I'm sorry to bother you, Mr Angelić, but I was wondering if I could maybe have your autograph?

Enter LEILA, *in a head-to-toe Jennifer Beals homage.*

LEILA. Leave him alone, Sasha, for God's sake! Sorry about him, we shouldn't let him off his leash in public.

MILI. That's okay. I only sign asscheeks I'm afraid, but if you're happy to bend over?

SASHA *undoes his belt and turns around.*

LEILA. Sasha!

SASHA *does himself up, laughing hysterically.*

MILI *stands, goes to leave.*

SASHA. Oh come on don't be like that! Here, do you want a cigarette?

MILI. I'm alright thanks. Apparently they're bad for you.

SASHA. Yeah well, so is landing on your face from a thirty-metre drop but that didn't stop you doing it.

Silence... Tension.

MILI *breaks a smile and lets out a little laugh.*

MILI. Alright, fine.

He takes a cigarette. The moment it touches his lips he spits it out in disgust as his mouth is filled with loose bits of tobacco.

SASHA *and* LEILA *burst out laughing.*

Enter MINA.

MINA. What, you never seen a 57 before?

She takes the cigarette, lights it and hands it back to him.

The three friends sit down, facing the water.

You just gonna stand there, or...?

MILI *sits down next to them.*

LEILA. Didn't fancy the party then, Iliya?

MILI. Mili.

LEILA. Huh?

MILI. It's Mili... My friends call me Mili.

SASHA. Oh... Are they on their way, or?

LEILA *pushes him.*

MINA. Sasha, be nice, for fuck's sake.

SASHA. Okay I'll stop, I'll stop.

SASHA *opens his bag, takes out a large bottle of flammable liquid and hands out some plastic cups. He offers one to* MILI.

MILI. I'm good, thanks.

LEILA. No one can see us down here, mate, the Shareef are all in bed by nine.

MILI. No I just... I don't drink.

SASHA. What?!

LEILA. Like, ever?

MILI....No.

LEILA. Not even before mosque?

MILI. My family's Catholic.

SASHA. Well then you definitely need a drink.

He holds the bottle out insistently.

MILI. Honestly, I'm alright.

SASHA takes a swig himself.

SASHA. This town will forgive you for a shit jump, Mili, but if they ever find out you don't drink, you'll be chased out with pitchforks.

MILI. Well I wasn't really planning on showing my face here ever again so they'd probably be doing me a favour.

LEILA. Come on, it wasn't that bad.

Silence.

SASHA bursts out laughing. The girls stare at him, unimpressed.

SASHA. I'm sorry, I tried... I really did.

MILI. It's alright. I'd be laughing too if my face didn't hurt so much.

SASHA. Mate, you've literally been here two minutes, what the hell were you thinking?

MINA. Sasha, can you just leave it, please? He can do what he wants.

SASHA. Oh, hi, Mina! Welcome back to the conversation.

MINA. Oh, piss off.

SASHA. I'm sorry about her, Mili, just before you embarrassed yourself in front of the whole town she *basically* told everyone she was in love with you, so –

MINA *and* LEILA. SASHA!

SASHA laughing whilst LEILA slaps his arm repeatedly. MINA walks off, dying of embarrassment.

LEILA. Come on, I'm taking you home.

SASHA. Wow, lucky you.

LEILA. Oh my God, you're SUCH A DICKHEAD!

SASHA. Goodnight, guys. Getting some mixed signals but I think I might have pulled.

She drags him off by the arm.

Have fun! Make sure you wear a –

LEILA *gags his mouth. Exit* LEILA *and* SASHA.

(Off.) IL-I-YA!… IL-I-YA!

Silence… It's painfully awkward. MILI *sits, trying not to laugh.* MINA *stands, back turned, waiting for the ground to swallow her.*

MILI. You just gonna stand there all night, or?

Listen, if you think that was the most embarrassing thing that's happened on this beach today you're not even close.

She takes a big breath in, composes herself and sits down.

Silence again. You can hear the crickets chirping.

What?!

MINA. I can hear you smiling!

MILI. I wasn't, I –

He tries not to laugh, but he can't stop smirking. She gets up to leave.

No! Okay, I won't, I promise. I promise…

She sits back down, feigning reluctance.

Silence.

MILI *looks up towards the sky.*

…It's beautiful from this angle, isn't it?

MINA. Eugh.

MILI. …Really? What now?

MINA. When people say 'it' it makes my skin crawl.

MILI. And what do you say?

MINA. I call her *she*. You do what you want.

Silence.

Endless silence.

MILI. Hey, so… fun fact, you know she is only two years younger than Shakespeare? How mad is that?

MINA. You're actually gonna sit there and explain my own bridge to me?

MILI. No! No, I didn't mean… I was just trying to…

Flustered, he takes a big breath in and checks his watch.

Look it's almost two, I should probably… I don't want to keep you from your friends if you're –

MINA. I like your watch.

MILI. Oh…

MINA. *Thank you?*

MILI. Sorry. Thanks… I saw it in this copy of *Vogue*, so…

They laugh.

MINA. It looks old. Where did you get it?

MILI. …Dad's.

MINA. He gave it to you?

MILI. Not really.

MINA. You stole it from him?

MILI. You lot ask a lot of questions.

MINA. And you don't answer any of them.

MILI. …He sold it. I got it back.

MINA. …Cool.

> *Silence.*

> (*Imitating.*) So fun fact, you know she's the same age as Shakespeare?

MILI. No way, really?

> *Laughter dispels the tension.*

MINA. …What are you doing here, Mili?

MILI. What happened to 'leave him alone, he can do what he wants'?

MINA. He can do what he wants, but she can still ask.

MILI. …Starting again.

MINA. And of all the places in the world to do that, you chose here?

MILI. What's wrong with here? This place is beautiful.

MINA. Are you joking? This is *literally* the most boring place in the world. Honestly, it's like time just broke one day and no one noticed. Like I walked past that shitty coffee shop on Liska [*Lee-ska*] Street the other day and I genuinely wondered if those old men out front just died and no one's ever thought to check. And whatever, you might think that's all cute and stuff but it actually makes me want to scream.

MILI. Well… where do you want to go and who's stopping you?

MINA. Okay so, I've narrowed it down to either Milan… or Paris… or New York. Or maybe London but only because, and like no big deal or whatever, but my auntie works in the British fashion industry so she could definitely get me a job there if I asked her to.

MILI. That's so cool. What does she do?

MINA (*hesitantly*). Oh, she works in like… you know, where they store all the clothes and stuff.

Silence.

Oh shut up, what about you then?

MILI. What about me!?

MINA. What are your big plans?

MILI.… When you make plans, God laughs.

MINA. Who said that?

MILI. I did.

MINA.… So no big dreams then? No ambitions?

MILI. Oh no, I've got plenty of those.

MINA.… Go on.

MILI. Find a job. Something with my hands, you know. Save up some money, fix the flat.

MINA. You got a place here?

MILI. Yeah, Mum's old apartment.

MINA. Your mum's from Mostar?

MILI. Was, yeah… Used to tell me stories about this town. Made it sound like a fairytale and I don't think she was too far off. What about yours?

MINA. Never got to meet her.

MILI. Shit. Sorry, I didn't mean to –

MINA. And when you finish the flat?

MILI. Well… I was hoping I might meet a nice girl… settle down… have some kids one day… raise them properly, you know.

MINA.… Well, Mili.

MILI.… Yeah?

MINA. I think you're gonna fit in this town just fine.

She stands up. Dusts her outfit down.

MILI (*laughing*). Are you calling me boring?

MINA. I am, yeah.

MILI....I'm sorry, did I say something wrong?

MINA. No. But just a bit of advice: if having kids is your big
ambition then you better check everything's still working
down there. You know... after all that.

She starts to leave.

MILI. Hey! Newsflash, Mina! Just because someone says they
want kids doesn't mean they want kids with you!

MINA....Oh. My. God. Who says 'newsflash' any more?

MILI. Listen, I was sitting here minding my own business,
okay? So don't make out like I was asking you to be part of
my life or whatever because I wasn't. I didn't make you sit
with me, I didn't make you ask me all these questions, and
I didn't laugh at you when you told me about 'Paris or Milan
or whatever' so don't be so stuck-up, okay?

*Silence. She walks up to him, staring right into his soul.
She's half the size of him and yet he's almost trembling.*

MINA. What did you call me?

MILI....Nothing. I said you're very friendly and I like your
dress. Is it Italian?

She smiles. So does he.

Look. You tell me this town's gonna be like this until the end
of time, then...

MINA. Then what?

MILI....Then maybe I've found everything I've ever wanted.

Silence.

He hesitates. Should he? Shouldn't he?

He leans in.

MINA *bursts out laughing.*

MINA. I'm sorry. I didn't mean to… it's just… you actually thought that was really smooth.

She goes to leave.

You coming or what?

Exit MINA.

MILI. Where?

MINA (*off.*) You owe me a coffee, don't you?

He thinks. He runs after her.

MILI. You joking? It's two in the morning!

Exit MILI.

1.5

Apartment, present.

As EMINA *narrates, her memories permeate through the space around her like ghosts captured in time. Each one flashing in and out to the sound of a Polaroid camera.*

EMINA. We climb back up those stone steps and head towards that shitty coffee shop on Liska Street. Two strangers just… talking, trying to make sense of each other's world. But as we get to Old Bridge, crossing together for the first time, I realise… I realise that I'm stood there talking to myself like an idiot.

I turn around and he's ten paces behind me, hand on the railing, staring at each step like it's a crossword puzzle. I walk back down towards him trying not to laugh.

MINA. Hey! Give me your hands. Both of them.

Back against the incline, she turns her body towards him and takes his hands in hers.

Look at me, don't look at the ground.

He does.

Toe first, heel second, okay?

MILI....Okay.

EMINA. I hold him. Guide him. Toe first. Heel second.

All.

The way.

To the top.

He lets go of me. Looks over to that spot he'd thrown himself off only hours ago and I can feel his heart sinking. A heart that told him you had a chance to belong somewhere again, and you blew it.

MINA. Hey... Come here, I want to show you something.

She runs up to the railings and climbs through them, facing out over the whole of Mostar.

MILI. Mina! Mina, what are you doing?!

He throws his arms around MINA's *waist and pulls her back against the rails.*

EMINA. I never felt someone hold on to me so tight. He tucks his chin against my shoulder as we look down, gazing into the pitch black beneath us like we're standing on the edge of the world.

MINA. Close your eyes.

MILI. Stop messing around, Mina, come on you're scaring me!

MINA. Hey... Trust me for a second, okay, just... close your eyes.

EMINA....As I take one of his hands and hold it out in front of me, I feel the other one pull me even tighter.

MINA....Can you feel that?

MILI....Feel what?

MINA.…The wind. Follow it with your hand.

He laughs.

Hey! Don't laugh, I'm being serious, listen…

The wind rattles against EMINA*'s window.*

It's the shape of the mountains. When it peaks like that you think it's passed, but there's always that one last…

The wind hits her window again, then subsides.

That's the bit that caught you…

MILI. Come on. You're making me nervous…

MINA. Okay, fine… but you'll have to let go of me first.

MILI *takes a step back. As he does, she puts her arms out in Lasta.*

MILI. MINA!

He launches towards her. MINA *puts her arms down and bursts out laughing. She climbs back through and throws her arms around him.*

…That wasn't funny.

MINA. Oh no trust me, that was funny!

EMINA. He tries to look all serious, but he can't help smiling as well.

…And when that laughter fades, we're just stood there. Staring at each other, silently. I want him to kiss me so bad.

'Mina…' he says.

MINA. Yes, Mili?

MILI. I was wondering if… would it be okay if I… would you mind if I took your photograph?

EMINA. No one had ever asked me that before… My eyes go wide as he rummages through his bag and takes out a Polaroid camera. I'd only ever seen one of these in movies.

I straighten the knot on my bow, flick my hair back and strike a pose. But he stands right next to me, holds the camera out at arm's length and takes a…

He stretches out his arm and takes a photo of the two of them.

Well I don't know what we called it, but they weren't called selfies then.

The machine churns as my eyes glow purple, gifting a little white square into his hands.

He passes it to her. She lets it rest in her open palms.

I stare at it like it's the most precious thing on earth. Watching as two little faces start to emerge. Two Hollywood stars… in another life perhaps.

MINA. Can I… can I keep this?

MILI. …Who did you think it was for?

She looks at him.

EMINA. And as I stand there looking into his eyes, that same burst of wind swoops down into the canyon and –

It snatches the photo clean out of her hands. Both of them launch up to the railings as they try to grab it. Silence as they watch it flutter off into the darkness.

My eyes well up. Sounds stupid, I know. I turn around thinking he's gonna be angry at me but he's just smiling… Lifts my chin up, meets my eyes, and –

MILI. Hey… come on, what's this?

MINA. Sorry. Sorry, I'm just being stupid.

She dries her eyes. Careful not to smudge her mascara.

MILI. We can take another one if you want?

MINA. …Really?

MILI. Of course we can. We can take as many as you like.

MINA. …I think I'd like that.

MILI. …I think I'd like that too. You're not in a rush, are you?

Silence.

EMINA. '…No' I tell him.

No, Mili, I'm not in a rush.

…We've got all the time in the world.

They look at each other…

They smile…

They lean in…

And kiss for the first time.

As their lips meet, the scene bursts into a Technicolor explosion of Boy Meets Girl's 'Waiting for a Star to Fall'. The air around them sparkles with the light of ten thousand perfect memories as their teenage love-lust makes the world stop spinning.

MILI *offers her his hand and she takes it.*

With childlike excitement they run head-first into:

PART TWO – Nevermind

2.1

Apartment, 1990.

The music continues; merging into the sound of the stereo.

SASHA *is on the sofa playing his guitar.* MILI *is sat at the dinner table with* LEILA, *who's flicking through their photo album. Everyone is smiling as though they'd just posed for a photograph. The camera churns as it dispenses a Polaroid into* MINA*'s hand.*

A basketball match plays on the television. MINA *drifts between her guests and the food she's preparing.*

SASHA. No way, I haven't heard this for years! Turn it up.

MILI *does.* SASHA *starts playing along.*

MILI. Aww, this was playing on our first date.

LEILA *and* SASHA *pretend to be sick.*

Yeah okay, okay…

LEILA. Mina, these photos are gorgeous. Seriously, how are we this cute?

The call-to-prayer starts.

SASHA. Let me see.

LEILA. I don't mean you!

MINA *turns the stereo off; music ends abruptly.*

SASHA. Oi, what you doing, I was listening to that!

MINA. Yeah well you're gonna have to wait two minutes, aren't you.

SASHA.…Is she taking the piss? I genuinely can't tell if she's joking or not.

MINA. I'm not *taking the piss*, it's just what you do, isn't it? My auntie did it for the neighbours, so –

SASHA. Well, she's not gonna hear you from England, is she?

He turns the stereo back on.

MINA *turns it back off.*

MINA. Sasha, we're right next to a mosque, can you just wait for like –

SASHA *plays on vigorously, making up the lyrics:*

SASHA. 'Waiting for Islam to call! I want her to turn the music on, but they're quoting the Quran in my – '

A guitar string snaps.

Silence but for the Adhan.

Divine intervention. SASHA *drops to his knees in prayer, reciting along with the muezzin in full vigour:*

Eshedu en la ilahe ille Allaaaaaah!

MINA. Sasha...

SASHA. Eshedu enne Muhammmmmad-en resul Allaaaaaah!

MINA. Sasha!

She clanks him on the head with the photo album. He stops, climbs back on the sofa and tends to the broken string, chuckling.

Pop this in there for me, babe.

MILI *finds a space for the Polaroid.*

LEILA. Look, Mina, no disrespect to your auntie but she didn't do it for the neighbours, she did it to impress the neighbours.

MINA. Hey!

LEILA. Oh come on, my mum's the same. No one wants to be the least Muslim Muslim in a room full of Muslims. Then the second we're alone – (*Points to the table.*) it's all pork mezze and plum brandy.

MILI. I've been to one of your weddings: nobody drinks but everyone leaves drunk.

LEILA. Oh don't you start laughing! If it was up to your lot we'd all be praising Jesus!

MILI. My lot? My mum's from –

LEILA. Yeah and what happened? She marries a Catholic, moves to Croatia and Hail Mary it's midnight mass and fish on a Friday.

MINA. It's not all bad; he got a flat out of it.

SASHA. Socialism, mate: we all got a flat out of it.

MILI. Is that why you never leave?

LEILA. Trust me, Mina, there'll be portraits of Mother Mary hanging from the walls by Christmas.

SASHA. She's not wrong, Mili. You've hardly been together two years and you've already dragged this sweet little Muslim girl to the Catholic side of town.

MILI. This isn't 'the Catholic side'.

MINA. And I'm not Muslim! Look, I'll turn it up, it's not a big deal.

SASHA. No no, it's fine. (*Pretending to whisper.*) Don't start oppressing her, Mili, that's when they radicalise.

I've seen it all before, mate. First the music goes, then the bacon's gone, next thing you know she's telling you to convert if you want a shot at marriage.

MINA. He knows the deal. I'm not marrying him until he wins a jump; the only thing he needs to convert is his awful Lasta.

LEILA. It's 'revert' actually.

SASHA. Excuse me?

LEILA. You don't *convert* to Islam, you *revert*.

SASHA. Jesus, not you as well? Run, Mili, before they circumcise the lot of us!

MILI. Use the prosciutto, it's like garlic to vampires!

SASHA *waves a piece of pork at* LEILA. *She stares at him, unimpressed. He eats it and laughs.*

LEILA. I honestly don't know why I'm friends with you.

SASHA. I know it's haram but it tastes so halal.

MILI. Erm, quick question, how is Sasha the only one here getting away without a roasting?

SASHA. Because I'm a half-Catholic, one eighth German, Roma Jew with a Muslim great-great-something or other, so if you can think of something witty enough then be my guest.

LEILA. That doesn't even make sense! Half of those cancel each other out, they're opposing ideologies!

SASHA. You're an opposing ideology.

LEILA *throws a cushion at him.*

MILI. So what exactly does that make you, Sasha?

SASHA. Mostar. Born and bred. And that's all that matters…

MINA. And a little bit German but we don't mention that.

The call-to-prayer ends. MINA *turns the stereo back on.*

SASHA. See, there she goes…

MINA. Oh, for God's sake!

SASHA. I'm on to you, Emina… And don't try any of that 'respect for your neighbours' crap, you're on the Croatian side now so you'll need a better excuse than that!

MILI. Sasha, this is not *the Croatian side*! Look, the Albaharis are downstairs; they're Jewish. The Petrović family are across the road; they're Orthodox Serbs. You practically live here, mate, which according to you brings a whole host of righteous diversity to the table. And okay granted there might not be *as many* Muslims on this side of Old Bridge, but in case you haven't noticed there's a bloody great big mosque outside my window! This town's like a… an infinitely tangled Rubik's Cube of religion; Jesus and Allah couldn't separate the colours if they booked off Lent and Ramadan!

Silence.

LEILA.…It's actually quite easy to solve a Rubik's Cube, it's basically an algorithm.

MINA. Babe. Read the room.

SASHA. No, she's right. It just takes one clever fucker to peel the stickers off and the fun's ruined for everyone.

MINA. Sasha, I'm not being funny but you spend all day learning how to stick your hand up a cow's arse. If it's a politics degree you're after, you're not gonna find one up there.

SASHA. Okay, first of all: everyone in this country is a bloody politician. And second, I don't stick my hand up cows' arseholes, okay?… I get my whole arm in. Right up to my shoulder, like that.

Laughter and disgust. MILI *tops up* SASHA*'s drink.*

MILI. I'm sorry, mate, I didn't mean to raise my voice.

SASHA. Hah! You call that raising your voice? Is your boy always this soft, Mina?

MINA. Always.

MILI. Look, these are weird times. The Bosnians are getting more Muslim, the Croatians are getting more Catholic, and the Serbs –

SASHA. Well, they never change.

MILI. No, that's exactly my point! When you make jokes like that, it just adds fuel to the fire, doesn't it? All this 'Catholic side, Muslim side' 'us and them' talk, it's starting to creep me out.

SASHA. A Bosnian and a Croatian get thrown out of a bar…

LEILA. Look, politics is a pendulum. Everything they're talking about, it's gonna pass.

SASHA. The Bosnian wouldn't order a drink, and the Croat wouldn't pay for one!

MINA. What's gonna pass?

SASHA. As in, your lot are tight and her lot pretend they don't drink? Come on!

MINA *takes a tray of burek out of the oven and plants it on the table: a traditional filo-pastry dish that's eaten like pizza.*

MILI. It's not a pendulum it's a wrecking ball… Too far in one direction and the party's over.

SASHA. And I guess Serbs don't really go to bars; they're too busy starting wars.

Disapproving groans.

LEILA. Sasha, what did he just say!

MINA. Come on, guys, you can't save the world on an empty stomach.

Standing around the table, they all dive in, hands into the tray.

Erm, excuse me!

They stop. Look at her. MINA *places a handful of cutlery on the table, and turns the TV off.*

SASHA. Burek with a knife and fork, you joking?

MINA *lights a candle, and looks at them patiently…*

Reluctantly they all sit around the dinner table. MINA *serves.* SASHA *flourishes his napkin extravagantly before placing it on his lap.*

MINA. Right. Alhamdulillah!

MILI. Amen!

They start eating.

LEILA. Babe, this is delicious.

MINA. Thank you!

SASHA. Yeah, you've absolutely smashed it.

MINA. Thanks, guys…

Eyes turn to MILI, *too immersed in his food to notice.*

LEILA. Anything to add there, Iliya?

MILI. Only spies talk when there's food.

SASHA. That reminds me, what do you lot think of the government? I'm asking for a friend.

Laughter followed by silence.

MINA.…Okay fine! If you want to move to the sofa –

A clamour of approval as LEILA, SASHA *and* MILI *drop their cutlery, pick their plates up and move to the sofa.*

Hold on, let me take a photo.

SASHA. Mina, can we turn the game back on?

He turns the TV on. MINA *searches for the camera.*

MINA. I swear to God I literally just… never mind, found it!

She primes the camera and points it at her friends.

Everybody smile!

No response – the camera clicks and flashes.

Guys?

None of them look up from the screen. MINA *lowers the camera and turns to see what they're watching.*

A news anchor reads in a language that's foreign to us; what she says is not important.

The screen illuminates them as they stare, transfixed in youthful ignorance. Four kids that could be anywhere, at any time, living that moment that happens once in every generation. That moment when everyone stops to listen. No one speaks, but everyone wonders: 'what happens now?'

SASHA *tries to change the channel but they all show the same picture.*

The newsreader's voice gets louder.

SASHA *tries to turn the volume down, but it keeps getting louder.*

He taps the remote control, tries to turn it down. Still nothing.

The reader's voice gets louder, and louder, and louder until it's piercing your ears with an almost wraith-like shrill. You want to cover your ears, but the moment you reach for them –

Silence. The kids disappear.

2.2

Apartment, past and present.

EMINA. The next morning I walk Leila back to hers. Neither of us saying a word. For the first time in my life I didn't recognise my home. Everything was exactly as it always was, and yet everything was different. I wave at Mr and Mrs Hasanović on the way back, sat out on their porch as they always were, but they didn't even blink. Eyes just glazed over in silence.

I head home as quickly as I can before the air outside starts suffocating me.

I get back to an empty apartment. The phone rings as it always did each Sunday at exactly noon. But as it pierces through the silence I nearly jump out of my skin. 'Inbound call from London, England. Press one to accept.'

Mili walks in with two bags of a shopping and a beaming smile. That's all it takes. The tension in my soul dissolves as everything feels normal again.

MINA *on the telephone.* MILI *has just entered. He starts unpacking groceries.*

MINA. No, he's doing alright yeah. Annoying... as ever, but someone had to take him.

The Ivanović factory, yeah... No they love him there, they just gave him shift supervisor... No, please, if I ask him he gets so excited and I...

What do you make again, babe?

MILI. So in plant machinery there are these pistons that need to be strong enough to –

MINA. Machines, yeah. He makes machines.

How's London?... Aww stop it, that sounds like a dream.

MILI *hands her a bottle of shampoo. She stares at it confused.*

I will... No you know I will soon, promise... Oh my God, really!? No...

Mili, did we get any packages?

MILI.…It's Sunday.

MINA. No, not yet. What was it?… Aww, you didn't have to… my birthday was weeks ago!

Oh… when did you send it?

Okay well… I'm seeing Leila tomorrow so I'll try the post office. It's probably just a… Yeah, she's alright.

No, that's fine, he's just got back too so I should probably… Yeah he's like a little puppy, if you don't give him enough attention he starts getting nervous.

Okay, I love you too, Auntie. I will yeah. Love you byeee.

She puts the phone down.

Oh hi.

MILI. Hi.

They kiss. She picks up the shampoo bottle.

Yeah sorry, it's the only one they had.

MINA. What do you mean?

MILI.…I mean, they didn't have your one so I got this.

MINA. But I don't like this one. Do you have the receipt?

MILI. It's shampoo, Mina, they're all the same.

MINA. Oh my God, you're such a…

MILI. What?

MINA.…Man!

MILI. You know what, I'm taking you back for a refund as well.

He lifts her up, she screams playfully.

MINA. Stop. Stop! Put me down! Mili!

He puts her down on the kitchen counter.

They kiss.

Do you know how lucky you are that you're so gorgeous?

MILI. Why's that then?

MINA. Because if you weren't you'd be completely useless.

MILI. Yeah and you'd be alone.

She hits him on the chest.

Do you want a coffee?

MINA. I just had one…

MILI.…Do you want another one?

MINA. Yeah.

He puts a pan of water on the stove. She picks up the shampoo bottle and examines it.

Hmm… what if it makes my hair all dry and flaky, are you gonna dump me?

He searches through the kitchen cupboards.

MILI. Not straight away. I'd wait a bit so people didn't think I was shallow.

MINA. Awww that's so sweet.

MILI. We're out of coffee. I'll be right back.

MINA. No I'll go, you just went.

MILI. It's fine, I'm dressed. Keep the water on, I'll be two seconds.

He heads towards the door.

MINA. I love you!

MILI. I know.

Exit MILI.

Lights.

EMINA. Three months pass… Still no package.

Sasha phones me after lectures, invites himself around. I tell him I need to grab some coffee so let yourself in if I'm not back. Ask him to try the post office for me on his way over; might as well put him to work. Oh and give Leila a call too, see if she's about.

I walk into the store and there's shouting coming from the back; two women fighting over a bag of pasta. Like actual grown-up women. Whatever reaction my body needed, my brain couldn't conjure. I just grab two bags of coffee and head towards the counter.

'Put that back!' she yells at me. So loud I almost jump out of my skin. 'It's one per customer!'

I want to scream right back at her but my lungs are empty. If I stay a moment longer I might catch whatever madness has infected them so I just throw my money on the counter and run towards the door.

Feel my blood boiling as I'm walking back. Everything I should've said is doing laps around my brain and I know that someone's head is gonna fly if the right person gets on the wrong side of me.

SASHA *is sat on the sofa with a bag of frozen peas pressed against his face.* LEILA *is stood next to him, tending to a cut above his eye.*

Enter MINA. *A bag of coffee in her hands.*

MINA. Sasha! What the hell happened?

SASHA.…They didn't have your package.

MINA. I'm sorry, is one of you gonna tell me what's going on?!

SASHA. I'm fine, Mina, relax.

MINA. You're not *fine*, Sash, you're bleeding. And don't tell me to relax!

She approaches him and inspects the cut.

SASHA. Honestly, it's nothing. They barely wrinkled my shirt.

MINA. They?! What do you mean *they*?!

LEILA. We're in the queue and these two meat-heads start arguing about God knows what. Before you know it one of them starts shouting 'This is Croatia!' The other one goes 'No, this is Serbia!' And then smart-arse over here says –

SASHA. Actually this is the post office.

He tries to laugh but he winces as his cheekbones move.

MINA. You need to learn to keep your mouth shut sometimes, you know that? Did anyone help? What did the staff do?

SASHA. Not much.

MINA. What? You mean they just…?! No, I'm sorry, this is bullshit! I'm going down there.

SASHA. No. No you're not!

LEILA grabs her arm.

LEILA. Babe! That's not gonna help anyone.

MINA pulls her arm free.

MINA. Oh it's gonna help me, big time!

She grabs her jacket and heads to the door.

LEILA. Mina! Take your jacket off and SIT DOWN!

Silence. They've never heard her shout before.

Enter MILI in his work overalls.

MINA. Mili?… Why aren't you at work?

MILI.…It was closed.

MINA. What do you mean, it was closed?

MILI. It was closed. The doors were bolted shut. Everyone was just stood outside.

MINA.…What did they say?

MILI. What did who say?

MINA. Anyone. Was there a manager there? Was there a sign?

MILI. There was a sign, yeah.

Silence. MILI's eyes are glazed over.

MINA. Hello! What did the sign say?

MILI.…It said closed.

He turns to SASHA.

What happened to you?

They disappear.

3 a.m. Darkness but for a small lamp. MILI *and* SASHA *talk quietly. Adhan from the nearby mosque.*

EMINA. Three months pass… Still no package.

For the first time in my life the call-to-prayer wakes me. It's 3 a.m. and I'm staring at the ceiling. The boys are in the other room talking. Sasha always thinks he's being quiet when he's had a drink, but I can hear every word.

SASHA. We can't just 'jump in a car', Mili, they've got checkpoints on every –

EMINA. Mili tells him to keep his voice down. He tries to listen but his words still creep through the walls. I bury my head between the pillows, try to force my eyelids shut, but this night wasn't meant for sleeping.

MILI.…Not loads. Just what I saved for the flat but –

SASHA. Mate, forget the flat!

MILI. It's not the money, Sash, I just don't have enough for four tickets.

SASHA. Listen to me. If you can get her out then don't even think twice. Small groups are easier, me and Leila can sort something out.

MILI. No. No, we need to stick together. I'm talking about two weeks out of town somewhere, not bloody London!

Glass shatters across the road as a brick is thrown through the mosque. SASHA *and* MILI *hit the floor. Enter* MINA *as she runs out of the bedroom.*

MINA. Mili?!

MILI. Shhhh! Get down!

MINA. Are you okay?

SASHA. We're fine! Come here.

MINA. What's going on?

SASHA *approaches the window, opens it carefully and looks outside. His face is illuminated in red as a petrol bomb is thrown into the mosque.*

SASHA. Shit!

The boys run for the door.

MILI. Stay here! Close the windows, turn off the lights!

Exit MILI *and* SASHA.

Lights.

EMINA. Three months pass… Still no package.

No school in Paris.

No job in London.

Piece by piece your world starts to change so you change with it. You hold on to whatever lies you need to get you through each day. And you're so good at deceiving yourself that you don't even realise it's happening. But you know deep down the moment's coming… the one that finally makes you crack. You just hope each morning that it's not today.

Enter MINA. *Half-asleep.*

Dawn's barely broken. I walk into an empty living room and the TV's on. No picture. Just white noise hissing quietly and no one watching.

I stare trance-like at the haze, still half-asleep.

MINA. Mili?

MILI (*off*)….Hey.

MINA….Where are you?

MILI (*off*). I'm on the roof. I think the antenna's broken. Can you see anything?

MINA….No. Sorry.

MILI (*off*)….What about now?

The signal flickers.

MINA….Still no.

MILI (*off*). Okay… alright, I'm coming down.

MINA. Can I do anything?

MILI (*off*). Yeah, you can put the coffee on.

EMINA. I put the water on the stove. Open the cupboard but we're out of coffee. I grab a jacket and the first pair of shoes I see.

Exit MINA.

I knock on Mrs Albahari's door, hoping she'll lend us some. No one answers.

Not a problem. Cross the road, pass the mosque, towards our little shop. Try the handle but the door is locked. I peer through the window. Shelves are empty. Lights are off.

No bother. I walk down towards the market. Pyjamas and heels. If anybody saw me dressed like this they'd think I'd lost my mind but there's not a single person on the streets and now I'm wondering if I've actually woken up at all. Stare at your feet. That's what they say. If you can't see your feet then you know you're dreaming but there they are… exactly where they always were.

They lead me to the market and but it's empty as well. Not a soul.

On a Sunday.

I think it's Sunday…

Maybe it's Saturday… I guess the Albaharis were at synagogue.

Old Bridge just past that corner there. I'm practically at Leila's anyway. Find a payphone. Dial the first number I learnt by heart.

MINA (*by a payphone*)….Hey, it's me. I'm just by yours, do you mind if I borrow some –

LEILA *is hiding under a table, shaking, clutching a landline.*

LEILA. Mina? Mina, you've got to help me, please!

MINA. What's going on, are you okay?!

LEILA. Mum's lost her fucking mind. She's screaming at me, she's saying we need to leave.

MINA. Leave? Leave where?

LEILA. I don't know! She's not making any fucking sense!
Listen, I need to stay at yours for a bit, please!

MINA. Hey, it's alright. It's alright. Look, I'm by Old Bridge,
just meet me next to –

LEILA. No! Go home, Emina! Don't wait for me!

Lights as LEILA *slams the phone down.*

EMINA. I stand there mid-sentence as my change tumbles
down the machine. Receiver still pressed against my ear.

Let the silence settle in.

That's when I heard it first…

That rumble in the sky.

…I take a big breath in. Conjure up my final ounce of
strength and surrender any claim to sanity that I have left:
I look up towards the sky and with a great big beaming smile
across my face I say 'Gee, it's a bit early for fireworks, isn't
it? Ramadan's not for another month.'

*Trying her hardest not to cry. She takes a big breath in, and
leaves.*

At the apartment SASHA *and* MILI *are talking.* MILI's
visibly nervous; in his hand is a gift from SASHA, *wrapped
tightly in a plastic bag.*

Enter MINA.

MINA. Hey.

The boys stand down. A look of relief across their faces.

You're being weird. What's going on?

SASHA. See. Nothing to worry about. I'll catch you lot later.

Exit SASHA.

MINA.…What was that about?

MILI. What do you mean?

MINA. What were you two up to?

MILI. …Trying to fix the TV.

He stuffs the gift into the kitchen drawer.

MINA. That's the first time you've ever lied to me. What's in the bag?

MILI. I'm sorry, are you gonna tell me where you've been or?

MINA. …I just popped out.

MILI. I know you 'just popped out' because I've been here pulling my hair out for two fucking hours!

MINA. Excuse me?

MILI. Where were you?!

MINA. I went to get us coffee! Is that okay with you?

MILI. You should've told me, you know I would've gone.

MINA. I'm perfectly fucking capable of buying coffee, okay!

MILI. …Well?

MINA. …Oh shut up!

She storms into the bedroom, comes back with a pile of bedsheets and throws them on the sofa.

MILI. What are you doing?

MINA. Leila's sleeping on our sofa for a bit. Her mum's being a dickhead as well.

MILI. No! Call her, tell her to stay where she is.

MINA. Mili! What's the matter with you?!

MILI. Listen to me… Phone her, tell her to stay until I come and get her.

Silence. MINA *just stares at him like he's a stranger.*

Fine, what's her number? Mina! What's her number?

The phone rings. They both race for it. MILI *gets to it first.*

MILI. Leila?! Oh… no, sorry. Yes. Yes she is. One second…
It's your aunt.

She snatches it from him.

MINA. Auntie, it's me… Hey, can you hear me? Hello?…
Hello?

MILI *takes the receiver from her and holds it by his ear.
Silence. He hits the button down repeatedly; tries to dial but
gets nothing.*

*He takes a moment, tries to breathe but the room is running
out of air.*

*He rips the phone out from the wall and slams it on the
counter.* MINA*'s scream echoes through the room.*

Silence as the shame consumes him.

…Mili.

*She walks over to him, slowly. Lift his head up, makes him
meet her eyes.*

Mili, look at me.

She holds him by the collar. Tiptoes. Kisses him slowly.

What's the matter? What's going on?

MILI. Nothing.

MINA. Hey. It's me, okay? Talk to me…

MILI. It's nothing. Honestly. Everything's under control, trust
me… I just need to –

She rushes to kitchen drawer and opens it as MILI *tries to
stop her.*

No, wait! Don't –

*She tears open the plastic package and finds a gun inside.
She lifts it out with both hands, studying it carefully as
though it fell from space. Then suddenly, as if it were
burning hot, she drops it into the drawer and slams it shut.*

Let me explain –

She turns the stereo on. 'Smells Like Teen Spirit' by Nirvana blasts into the room. She starts laying the bedsheets out.

Hey! Are you listening to me?

She turns it up, loud.

Mina!

He puts his hands on her shoulders and she stops; the weight of it finally breaks her. She turns around and looks at him, eyes full of tears.

MINA. Mili, I'm so scared.

He hugs her. Tight.

MILI. I know... I am too, but I'm not gonna let anything bad happen to us, okay? Never. I promise.

He kisses her.

Enter LEILA, *bag in hand, shaking. Covered head-to-toe in a thick layer of dust and debris.*

MINA. Leila!

MILI. Shit. Come here! Sit down. Get her some water.

MINA *tries to fill a glass from the tap but nothing comes out.*

Leila, can you hear me? Leila? What's happened? Mina, we really need some water!

MINA. I'm trying, there's nothing coming out!

LEILA (*dazed*). I'm sorry... I can't... what?

MILI. For God's sake, can you turn off the –

The power cuts out.

Music stops.

MINA *opens the curtains to let some light in and stands transfixed by what she sees: in the near distance a metal behemoth cranes its neck towards her slowly, as it takes aim at their mosque.*

Hey… come over here…

Mina, get away from the window…

Minaaa!

He grabs MINA *and* LEILA *and drags them both to the floor.*

A flash.

Blackout.

White noise.

PART THREE – Let's Hear It for the Boy

3.1

Darkness.

From the minaret of a nearby mosque, the Adhan is heard. As the muezzin calls Muslims to prayer, it's hit by tank fire. The sound of the Adhan slows, like a cassette tape churning in a broken stereo. Another explosion finishes it off.

The sound of the tower collapsing, falling onto a row of houses.

Lights up.

Apartment, December 1992.

The ruins of their home. A candle is all that spares them from total darkness. There's no electricity, the windows have been barricaded, and everything is so filthy you can smell it.

SASHA *plays '(I've Had) The Time of My Life' by Bill Medley and Jennifer Warnes quietly on his guitar.* LEILA *is sat next to him while* MILI *and* MINA *practise a dance routine that she's clearly choreographed.*

MILI *does a misstep.*

Everyone trying to whisper:

MINA. Mili! Do it properly!

MILI. I did! That's exactly what you –

MINA. No it wasn't! How many times: Left, left, right, left, spin!

   A shell lands nearby. Everyone ducks.

SASHA. Drink!

   MINA, SASHA *and* LEILA *do a shot.*

   SASHA *gets up and fills their glasses, swaying a little.*

LEILA. Do the lift!

MINA. Yeah!

MILI. Nope. No way.

LEILA. Go on! You've haven't done it for years.

MILI. Yeah, for a reason.

MINA. Please! I won't mess it up, just – Shit, Sasha!

SASHA topples over. MILI catches him. Laughter.

LEILA. Pretty sure it didn't look like that in the film.

MINA. This is your own fault, you know that.

SASHA. It might be my fault... but it's your problem.

MILI. Okay, mate, bedtime, let's go.

MILI slings him over his shoulder.

SASHA. No! I'm fine... Where's my hat?

MINA. Shit, Mili, what's the time?

LEILA. Found it.

She puts SASHA's hat on him: a handmade paper cone hat with '1993' written across it.

MILI. Quarter to midnight.

LEILA. Wait... mine says twenty to one?

Silence. They don't know what to do.

SASHA....Fuck it!

ALL. Five! Four! Three! Two! One! (*Whispering.*) Happy New Year!

A shell lands nearby. Everyone ducks.

SASHA. Drink!

MINA and LEILA do a shot. Over MILI's shoulder, SASHA picks his glass up from the table and pours it into his mouth.

MINA. No! No, no, no, no, Sasha!

MILI. What?!

As MILI spins to try and see, he stumbles, knocking the candle over.

Blackout.

3.2

Apartment, November 1993.

From the darkness, EMINA *enters.*

EMINA. 'When you make plans, God laughs.'

...When he first told me that, I laughed at *him*. But oh how I hated when he was right.

One day all you care about is music, fashion, and boys. The next day there's no food.

You come back from the shop, upset because they've run out of your favourite shampoo. A year later and there's bodies on the street... You look back at that version of yourself, that princess, and you barely recognise her.

'Not in my country.' That's what she used to say. Not in *Europe*. Not when Mariah Carey has been number one for four weeks straight!

A shell lands nearby. MINA *jolts up off the sofa.*

Lights up on SASHA *and* LEILA, *sat at the table playing cards by the candlelight.*

LEILA. Shhh, it's alright, hun, go back to sleep.

SASHA. Don't worry, mate, you won't hear the one that kills you.

MINA *sits back, breathing deeply as she takes in the room.*

EMINA. How could you not laugh at yourself? At everything...

You choose to laugh, or you choose to be a victim. It's as simple as that.

SASHA. You heard about that boy crossing Liska Street?

LEILA....No?

SASHA. Sniper. Shot him in the little finger and... he didn't make it.

LEILA. What? How did that kill him?

SASHA. It was up his nose when they fired.

She slaps him on the shoulder, but she can't help laughing.

LEILA. You're going to hell, you know that?

SASHA. Don't, please. You know what I'd give for a holiday right now?

EMINA. The first one makes you cry. The second makes you sad. The third one barely registers, and just like that... you discover an immunity you wish you never knew you had.

When Dina in the year above got shot in the neck fetching water I cried my eyes out. I barely knew the girl but I was inconsolable.

When Leila's block of flats got torched I felt my insides curdle as she screamed out for her mother. Soldiers with beaming smiles shooting women in their nightgowns as they ran into the street... Her mum treated me like I was one of hers but I don't think I cried. I just held Leila as she wept, wiped her tears and told her she lives here now.

I can't even remember who was third...

Mr Hasanović got dragged out of his bed in the middle of the night and I barely even blinked. Seventy years old. They didn't even waste a bullet on him, they just –

She takes a big breath in.

Can you feel that? Can you feel how that last one hurt less than the others? That's your immunity growing, and it's even stronger when you're living in it.

If it's not someone you love... If it's not someone you *need* –

SASHA. Hey! Staring at the door isn't gonna help.

MINA. He said he'd be two hours... it's been three.

LEILA. None of that face, okay? He'll be fine.

MINA. Oh, he told you that as well, did he?

SASHA. Only the good die young. And he's a bit of a bell-end, isn't he?

A shell lands outside. The silence it leaves is deafening.

SASHA *puts his cards down, picks up his guitar and starts playing 'How Will I Know' by Whitney Houston.*

MINA. Sasha, please…

He keeps playing.

No seriously, Sasha, I'm not in the –

SASHA *sings the first line of the song.*

MINA *tries her hardest not to smile.* SASHA *takes it up a notch, singing the second line.*

MINA *starts laughing.*

EMINA. The last thing you ever expected was to find beauty in those days… But soon enough you come to understand that laughter is the only weapon you have. Shells rain down from the skies in torrents, snipers line the mountains shooting anything that moves, but he'd run halfway across town dodging both because he heard a rumour that someone somewhere had a spare set of nylon guitar strings.

I hated him for it. I'd bang my fists against his chest and beg him not to go out there again. But he knew something that it took me a lifetime to understand…

You could go weeks without food, days without water. But a handful of coffee… a packet of cigarettes… or a pair of batteries for the stereo. Without these things your soul would starve to death, and that was a fate worse than any bullet. Any shell through your roof. Or any knock on your door if someone somewhere heard a rumour that you were hiding Muslims on the wrong side of town.

Even if two minutes ago… they barely felt like they were Muslim at all.

EMINA *fades.*

Knocking on the door.

Like a reflex, SASHA *grabs* MILI's *gun,* MINA *picks up a kitchen knife and hides behind a wall, and* LEILA *runs into the bedroom closing the door: a formation they've drilled a hundred times.*

Knocking on the door.

SASHA *moves towards it, braced.*

Knocking on the door.

SASHA *open it and aims.*

Enter MILI. *The room exhales.*

MILI. Sorry… lost my keys.

MINA *runs to him, hugs him, punches him on the chest then hugs him again.*

MINA. I swear to God if you ever lose them again I'll kill you myself!

SASHA. Shhhh!

MILI. Where's Leila?

LEILA. Mili?

MILI. I need to talk to you.

He can't find the words.

LEILA. Spit it out, you're scaring me!

MILI. …Leila, your mum was at the handout.

LEILA. What?

MILI. She got out…

LEILA. Don't… Don't fuck with me, Mili!

MILI. I'm not!… I wouldn't… She got across the river. She's been at her brother's for months.

Tears run from LEILA*'s eyes.*

When I told her you were alive… that you were here, with us… she just… she just…

LEILA. …What did she say?

He hesitates.

…Hello? What did she say?

MILI. I lost her. I'm sorry.

LEILA. What do you mean, you lost her?

MILI. We got separated, that's all, but she's fine. I promise, we just –

LEILA. Wait, wait, sorry, you got separated in a bread line?

MINA. …Something happened.

MILI. No it didn't.

LEILA. Yes it did… Yes it did, Mili, and you've got five seconds to tell me or I'm gonna go find out for myself!

SASHA. Guys, I'm not fucking about! Any louder and we're all in serious shit!

Silence.

MILI. …They fired on the handout.

LEILA. What?!

MILI. They ambushed the truck, they knew it was coming. She ran. We all did. I'm sorry, I didn't want you to –

LEILA. Was she hurt?

MILI. No, I don't think so.

LEILA. You don't *think* so?!

MILI. They didn't get her!

LEILA. How?! How can you know that?

MILI. Because I stayed to –

MINA. What do you mean you stayed?!

MILI. I had to hide, Mina, we didn't know where it was coming from! Everyone was on the ground, screaming. I'm shouting at this kid across the street, telling him to run but he's dropped all his tins and they just –

LEILA. I don't care about some fucking kid, Mili, just tell me she's okay!

MILI. Nine bodies… Nine. She wasn't one of them.

LEILA. …And you're sure?

MILI. Yes, Leila. Believe me, I got a pretty decent look!

MINA *goes to hug her but she pulls away.*

LEILA. Don't... touch me, please. I'm alright, just... give me a minute.

She heads towards the bedroom. MINA *tries to follow.*

Mina!

Exit LEILA, *alone.*

Silence.

MINA *looks at* MILI. *He opens his arms and holds her tight.*

MILI. I didn't mean to... I didn't want her to worry, that's all.

MINA. Are you hurt?

MILI. I'm fine, I just... that was someone's kid.

SASHA. Yeah well someone should've taught their kid to listen.

MINA. Sasha, for fuck's sake!

MILI. Come on... you need to eat.

He takes a plastic bag out of his backpack and hands it to MINA.

SASHA. What did you get?

MINA. Two loaves... Two tins of... something. Half a bottle of – (*Sniffs it and winces.*) paint-stripper.

She passes it to SASHA *who takes a swig.*

A bit of sugar, and...

Silence. She stares at MILI.

...coffee.

They hold eyes.

How did you – ?

MILI. Come on. Before our guests die of hunger.

SASHA. You guys eat. Rotation's in an hour, I should probably –

MINA. Have a bite at least? We've got – (*Opens a tin.*) tuna…
gross.

SASHA. I'm good, honestly. They'll feed me at work.

He puts his jacket on; green military issue.

But I wouldn't say no to a little aperitif.

He grabs two glasses from the kitchen and fills them up.

MINA. Oh… you know what, I'm alright. Think I'm gonna try
to lay off the booze for a bit.

SASHA, *aghast.*

SASHA.…This is your doing, isn't it!

MILI. Don't look at me, it's the first I've heard of it!

SASHA. Whatever. Suit yourselves.

He knocks both shots back.

I'm gonna sneak back over on Thursday, do you lot need
anything?

MILI. Actually…

He takes him aside whilst MINA *prepares dinner.*

I'm trying to get a hold of something.

MINA. What are you two whispering about?

SASHA. How many times, I'm not getting you porn!

MILI. Listen, her aunt's old house across the river… I think
there's still some tins left in the basement.

SASHA. And what do you really want?

MILI.…A box of Polaroids in the kitchen.

SASHA. You're joking, right?

MILI. Just, if you get there before I do. Please. It would make
her so happy.

SASHA. You take the piss sometimes, you know that?

They rejoin the room. SASHA finds his cigarettes, counts them, and leaves the box on the counter.

Here. Might come in handy.

MILI *picks them up.*

MILI. 57s? Could've gone a bit more upmarket.

SASHA. If I had anything nicer do you think I'd give them to you?

He picks up his rifle and slings it over his shoulder.

MILI. Sash, I can't take these.

SASHA. Yes you can.

MILI. Mate, there's four here. Two each?

He holds out two cigarettes.

SASHA. One... for the commute.

SASHA *takes one and lights it.*

MILI. You heard the latest? Apparently they're bad for you.

SASHA. Only thing keeping me alive.

He hugs them both.

MINA. How did you get across?

SASHA. Why do think I only had four left?

MINA. Alright, just... be careful, okay?

SASHA. Thanks, Mina, I... I didn't think of that.

MINA. Oh piss off.

SASHA. Right... I'll see you guys later. Keep your heads down.

He knocks on the bedroom door.

Hey... It's me. I'm heading off. Can I open the –

The door opens. Enter LEILA, fully dressed, bag in hand.

Silence, followed by realisation.

MILI. Leila, don't even think about it.

MINA. No… No, you can't!

LEILA. Sasha, I need to get across the river.

SASHA. Where does your uncle live?

LEILA.…Zalik.

MINA. Oh God.

MILI. You're joking? Leila, they've practically flattened it!

LEILA. Don't yell at me, please! I know what I'm doing, okay!
    If she's alive I need to –

MINA. You need to not get yourself killed!

LEILA. Mina, I've been sleeping on your floor for two fucking
    years. Two years! Eating your food when there's barely
    enough for the two of you!

MINA. I don't mind! Mili, tell her we don't mind!

LEILA. Look, anything that can happen to me over there can
    happen here, too, okay? If she's alive then I have to be with
    her. If that's not worth risking my life for then why the fuck
    am I trying to stay alive at all?

SASHA. She's right, guys.

MINA. Oh, you think this is a good idea, do you?

SASHA. What I think is she can do what she wants. And I'd
    rather she went with me than wandered off by herself.

MILI. Have you both lost your minds? Are you actually
    listening to the words you're saying? We're safe here. We
    just need to wait –

SASHA. For what? For the fucking cavalry to arrive? Don't
    hold your breath. You think anyone out there is losing sleep
    over this?

    You know what your boy just asked me to get you, Mina?

MILI. Sasha…

SASHA. A box of film. A box of fucking film somewhere in your old place, and you know what? The thought of seeing you smiling like that and I'll gladly let a sniper try stick one up my arse. So don't either of you try to tell me with a straight face that it's too dangerous to go see her mum.

You know why they turned the water off, don't you? It wasn't so you die of thirst, Mina, it's so your lot can't pray! But I'll tell you what, all those bodies lining the riverbank, trying to rinse their armpits so God starts listening again, do you think they've got any regrets? I don't. I think they died with a great big fucking smile on their faces and you can't ask for more than that now, can you?

...I'm not gonna lie to you, Mili, two each is starting to sound like a real good offer.

MILI *gives him a cigarette.* SASHA *tries to light it but he's out of gas, trembling with nerves.*

For fuck's sake!

MILI. I got it... I got it.

MILI *strikes a match and lights* SASHA*'s cigarette; he inhales deeply and is instantly calmer.*

LEILA. Mina...

MINA.... Yeah?

LEILA. The second this is all over, you know what we're gonna do?

MINA. What?

LEILA. We're gonna go to that shitty coffee shop on Liska Street, just me and you. Sit outside on those crappy plastic chairs and we're never gonna leave.

MINA.... You promise?

LEILA. Look at me, babe... All I've ever done my whole life is live in your footsteps. I love you, and I always will, but this is my choice now. Probably the only one I've ever made so for better or for worse I've made it, okay? So yeah, I promise... Come here.

They hug.

And now I don't have to pretend to be asleep when you two are having sex every night.

MINA. Leila!

They laugh.

SASHA. Guys.

LEILA….Right. Sorry.

MINA. No goodbyes, yeah? Just… I'll see you later.

LEILA. Okay… I'll see you later.

MILI.…See you later.

SASHA. See you later.

Exit LEILA *and* SASHA.

Silence.

MINA *and* MILI *look at each other. She launches herself into him, holding on with all her strength as tears run down her face.*

They hold each other for a lifetime.

MILI. Hey… I got you something.

He goes into his jacket pocket, takes out two large batteries and puts them in her hand.

MINA. What! How did you – ?

MILI. Don't worry about that.

MINA.…Can I?

MILI. Go on.

A moment.

She unplugs the stereo from the wall, discards the power cable, and puts the batteries in. She roots through the drawer, taking her time to find exactly the right cassette. She finds it, inserts it, and presses play.

'Girls Just Want to Have Fun' blares out at high volume.

MILI *jumps for the volume and turns it down immediately. He stares at her, unimpressed.*

MINA. Sorry!

She roots through the drawer again and finds her old headphones. She plugs them into the stereo, puts them on, and turns the volume up to her heart's content.

We hear the music as she does.

MINA. [Can you hear anything?]

MILI. [No… you're good.]

MINA *nods, smiles, closes her eyes and enjoys the music.*

She kisses him.

MINA. [Thank you.]

She takes the headphones off and presses stop. The sound of shelling and gunfire returns.

MILI. You're welcome.

She picks up a slice of bread, takes a bite and smiles at him.

MINA. You fancy a coffee?

MILI. You serious?

MINA. You want to try sleep through this?

She goes to the kitchen and pours some water into a džezva from an old cola bottle and places it on a canister of camping gas.

MILI. Mina, we're gonna be wide awake till dawn.

MINA.…I think I'd really like that.

She goes up to him and holds her hand out. A moment. He hands her the box of matches. She kisses him on the cheek, takes the matches and lights the camping stove.

They sit together on the floor and wait for the water to heat.

What time is it, anyway?

MILI.…Around two I think.

MINA. You think? Where's your watch?

Silence.

…Mili? No… you didn't?

MILI. Don't be angry, please…

MINA. For the batteries?

MILI. No… for the coffee, too.

She wants to be angry with him but she can't.

MINA. As soon as this is over… As soon as they've finished, I'm gonna buy you a new watch. I promise.

MILI. Hey, look at me… Look at me.

She does.

I don't need a new watch, I don't need anything, okay. I just need you. You're the only thing I care about, and all of this… all of it, is easier to endure than a life where I never met you. You know that, don't you?

She kisses him.

She kisses him passionately.

EMINA. Coffee, music, food on the table, and him… just him; the first time we'd been alone in months.

And for all the pain that those days brought… you're not capable of loving anyone as much as when you know that any moment you might lose them. Your body overtakes you. That person becomes a drug to you, and you're addicted to every ounce of them.

I would've given every happiness I'd ever had to spend a second longer in that moment.

Banging on the door.

MILI *grabs his pistol.* MINA *grabs the knife and hides.*

As MILI *walks towards the door:*

SASHA (*off*). Mili!

MILI. Shit!

EMINA. But... for reasons you can never understand...

He puts the pistol back in the drawer.

SASHA (*off*). Mili! Open the fucking door!

EMINA. Hell has chosen your little town for a summer holiday.

MILI *opens the door.*

Enter SASHA *carrying* LEILA *in his arms. There's blood everywhere. Her mouth is gagged to stop her screaming.*

Trying their hardest to keep their voices down:

MILI. What happened?!

SASHA. What the fuck do you think happened!

EMINA. And he liked it here so much he decided to stay.

MILI. Put her down. Put her down! Leila, can you hear me?

She cries through a mouth stuffed with cloth. MILI *goes to take it out but* SASHA *grabs his hand.*

SASHA. If she screams, we're all dead.

MILI....Fuck's sake!

SASHA. Mina, towel, whiskey!

EMINA. So however beautiful a moment you could savour...

Nothing. Frozen.

MILI. Mina!

Still nothing.

MILI *lifts* LEILA's *shirt up to see the wound. It's too dark; he lights a match and sees the hole in the side of her stomach.* LEILA *cries silently in pain.*

I know! I know, but you need to be brave, okay. Can you do that?

She nods, tears streaming from her eyes.

EMINA. He was always there with you... Waiting.

MILI. It's gotta come out.

SASHA. Are you fucking crazy?

MILI. It's lead, Sasha, if it stays in there…

SASHA.…Shit.

> MINA *turns around, curls into the corner and covers her ears.*

> LEILA *lets out a cry of pain.*

> MINA, *shaking, grabs the headphones, puts them on and presses play. 'Girls Just Want to Have Fun' plays loudly into her ears and all we hear is music. No bullets. No bombs. No screams. Nothing.*

> MILI *and* SASHA, *scared and out of their depth, try their hardest to save* LEILA's *life.*

EMINA (*shouting over the music*). And the reason it doesn't hurt you at the time… The reason you don't process the pain like a normal human being… it's not because you're a monster… It's because the horror of it all would be enough to kill you. Bring you back to life and kill you again ten thousand times each day. That immunity you hated yourself for… it's the only that that's keeping you alive…

But it comes with a price.

> *The song finishes. In the silence between tracks* MILI *shouts:*

MILI. Don't let her fall sleep!

SASHA. Leila! Leila, stay with me, mate!

> *The next track starts: 'We Don't Have to Take Our Clothes Off' by Jermaine Stewart – and once again we hear nothing else.*

> SASHA *pulls the towel out of* LEILA's *mouth, lifts her head and slaps her, hard and repeatedly on the side of the face.* LEILA *mumbles something.*

> SASHA *puts his cheek against her mouth.*

[She's not breathing. She's not breathing!]

SASHA *climbs on top of her and starts chest compressions.*
He pinches her nose, tilts her chin up and does two rescue
breaths.

Chest compressions. Rescue breaths.

As EMINA *speaks, the song starts churning through the*
cassette player, slow and reverberated in a minor key, as
though sung by a chorus of ghosts.

EMINA. And that's the bit that no one tells you… that they
come for you eventually. The ghosts, I mean. They find you
later and they scream for you, they say 'Why didn't you cry
for me!? Why didn't you *feel* anything!?' You beg them to
leave you alone but there's hundreds of them. Each waiting
patiently for their turn. Each waiting for you to pay them
back the debt of tears you owe them. Waiting for you to give
them what you didn't have then, and you're shouting because
you can't hear yourself think, shouting just to hear your own
thoughts and when they don't leave… that's when you start
asking for help. Praying to someone who you never believed
in before and begging for silence, that's all you ask for…

That's all you'll ever ask for the rest of your life.

Chest compressions. Rescue breaths.

MILI. [Sasha.]

SASHA *ignores him and continues: chest compressions,*
rescue breaths.

[Sasha…]

Losing his rhythm from exhaustion: chest compressions,
rescue breaths.

[Sasha!]

MILI *puts his hand on* SASHA*'s shoulder and tries to make*
him stop.

SASHA *jumps up and pushes him away violently.* MILI
trips, crashing over next to MINA.

MINA. [Mili!]

As she runs to him, she yanks the headphones out of the socket. The chorus blasts into the room at full volume, in its full natural vigour.

SASHA, MINA *and* MILI *all leap at the stereo.* SASHA *gets to it first and hits stop.*

Silence…

Only breathlessness and panting.

Eventually SASHA *stands up, wipes his tears, and starts getting dressed.*

SASHA. You need to get her out of here, Mili, your people are gonna be here any minute.

He goes into the bedroom and returns with a once-white bedsheet. He places it next to LEILA*'s body and rolls her into it, wrapping her up. Slowly it turns more and more red.*

I need to go. Can't be late for work now, can I?

SASHA *slings his rifle and sips the last drop of whiskey from the empty bottle.*

You got the time there, Mili?

Of course you don't. You sold your watch for a bottle of whiskey.

…Just like your dad.

MILI *launches himself at* SASHA*, grabbing him by the throat and drawing his fist.*

MINA. STOP IT!

He does. SASHA *hasn't flinched, smiling as* MILI *is consumed in shame.*

SASHA.…There he is. THERE HE IS!

MILI *lets go.*

You people are all the same deep down, aren't you? You may as well have just shot her yourself!

MINA. SASHA!

SASHA. Just tell your lot to go easy on her, yeah?

He looks at LEILA's *body, and takes a big breath in.*

I wanted to be a vet, Mina... a fucking vet.

He leaves.

MILI.... We need to go. We need to leave right now.

MINA *stares, frozen, at* LEILA's *body.*

MINA. I can't.

MILI. Look at me. Don't look at anything else, okay? Just me.
Please.

She does.

We need to cross the river. Your aunt's house, the basement.
They're shelling that side like crazy but it's all we got. Grab
your passport, grab your jacket, and when we're out there
you don't let go of my hand. You run when I tell you to run,
you stop when I tell you to stop, but if I get hit –

MINA. Mili!

MILI. Listen to me! If I tell you for whatever reason that *I can't
go any further*, you let go immediately, and you run. You do
not stay with me. You do not try to help me. You don't even
say goodbye. You just run, and you keep running. The only
time you ever stop is when the wind stops blowing.

A shell lands outside.

You hear that? Listen to the wind. You taught me that when
we first met and it's saved my life a hundred times.

MINA. The shape of the mountains.

MILI. Exactly. But when you get to Old Bridge you don't stop
for anything, you understand? If you can see the mountains,
they can see you, so don't make it easy for them. Just run, as
fast as you can.

Toe first, heel second, yeah?

She laughs through her tears.

MINA. I think I can remember that.

MILI. I thought so. Now get your things.

> MINA *goes into the bedroom.* MILI *puts his coat on, tears up the loaves of bread and stuffs each piece into his pockets.*

> MINA *re-enters, dressed.* MILI *goes into the bedroom.*

> *When he comes back she's clutching their photo album between her arms.*

MILI. Leave them.

MINA. No.

MILI. Leave them!

MINA. I can't!

MILI. Listen to me, they're all up here! All of them! And when we get through this we're gonna take hundreds more, okay?

> *She lets him take the album from her.*

Whatever happens… I'll find you, I promise.

> *One last kiss.*

> MILI *heads towards the kitchen drawer and finds his passport; as his back is turned* MINA *takes one Polaroid out of the album and slips it into a small gap in the floorboards. He heads to another drawer to get his gun, but as he does the door of the house is kicked in.*

> *A metal cylinder the size of a fist is thrown in through the door. The room is engulfed in a flash of blinding light. You can't see. You can't hear.*

EMINA. The taste of blood fills my mouth as I feel my face jolt to its side. I run my tongue against my cheek and find a gap where seconds ago a tooth had been.

> Eyes glow purple as the room is filled with torchlight.

MINA. Mili?!

EMINA. 'Shut the fuck up! Either of you move and I'll blow your fucking brains out.'

It rings in my ears. Can't tell if it's near or far. Two sets of boots are standing next to me, arms linked through my elbows as they lift me to my feet. I didn't even realise I was on the floor.

They turn their flashlights off. MILI *and* MINA *become visible, backs against the wall on opposite sides of the room.* EMINA *between them.*

The candle next to Mili is the only thing that spares us from the darkness, and I can see a fear in his eyes that I have never seen before.

They search us. I can smell the one in front of me. Feel the damp from his breath against my neck as he runs his hands through me. Takes his time with it. Finds our passports. Hands them over. Checks Mili's first.

'Dubrovnik?' he says. Looks at his colleague. 'You guys might know each other.'

He opens mine. Studies it then studies me. 'Oh… well, that is interesting. We heard you guys were having a little party. You don't mind if we join you?'

He walks over to me. Feel his coarse fingers as they stroke my cheek. He runs his hand between my legs. Pulls at me, hard, and I wince in pain.

MINA. Please!… I… I think I'm pregnant.

EMINA. Mili's eyes go wide. The man takes a step back.

'Oh… you should've told me sooner. Now I get to fuck two Muslims at once.'

MILI. Mina… I can't go any further.

EMINA. The soldiers just laugh. 'What a fucking hero.'

I look at Mili and I beg him not to but that fear in his eyes has gone. The man picks up Sasha's cigarettes. Takes one between his fingers and both of us can tell he's never seen a 57 before.

Mili's hand moves towards the kitchen drawer and I know exactly what's inside.

And the second that cigarette touches the soldier's lips…

Time stands still.

MILI *knocks the candle over and the room is immersed in darkness.*

Blackout.

Gunshots.

Screaming. Running. Bodies hitting the floor.

Door slams.

Jawbones cracking as fists land on human flesh.

Screams of pain.

Until…

Until this Bosnian word that's difficult to translate: 'pokosili' – the verb a farmer might use to cut down a field of wheat. Used to describe homes that were raided… 'Mow' comes close.

The sound of an automatic rifle mowing down a room.

Muzzle lights blind you.

Your ears ring.

They keep ringing.

They never stop.

3.3

Mostar, 9 November 1993. Dawn.

Calm. Silence. Just for a moment.

EMINA. The first time I ever left the house without heels on.

Any other day and I could tell you who, from my street to the riverbank, would be sat where and doing what. You could set your watch by them... If you had one.

But not today.

All life is gone... and I am the last living thing on this earth.

An explosion cracks like thunder as the tranquillity ruptures.

Shattered glass cuts my feet to pieces as I run. Run to Old Bridge leaving bloody footprints though the streets. Keep running, praying any moment now I'll see the town I'm looking for. Blue skies and cobbled streets. That any minute now –

Explosion as a shell lands nearby. Restless breathing echoes between your ears as the ringing settles.

Open my eyes. Look down. Touch my face. Touch my chest. Breathe in. I'm fine... Get up. Keep running. Run to Old Bridge, just like he said, don't stop. Dawn starts to break. Need to hurry. If you can see the mountains, they can see you. Turn right on Liska. Running. Running. Running. Wind stops. Find cover.

Silence... Explosion.

Breathe in. Breathe out. Knees cut on broken glass but I'm okay. Wind starts. Don't stop now. Keep going. Burnt stone stings the nostrils. Smells so thick it chokes me. Stay between the houses. Daylight's coming, run. Run down Liska, take a left towards –

Explosion. She ducks.

Our shitty coffee shop... White plastic chair-legs stick out from the rubble like a makeshift grave; marks the place where Leila's promise died.

Three kisses of sniper fire, she ducks.

Don't stop. Don't stop, this isn't where you die.

Run through the market. Feet screaming out in pain, don't stop, need to beat the sunrise. Running. Old Bridge, just past that corner there, keep going. Turn left towards the river, running, running, need to beat the sunrise, stop…

Silence… Peace.

Breathe in. Deep.

There she is…

Bruised and beaten. But alive…

The only other living thing in this whole town.

I try to remember Mili's words but they're a distant haze. I should be running but ten thousand memories weigh my ankles down. These hands and feet are no longer mine. Legs start gliding forwards on their own, fingers run along her walls through bullet holes and broken stone.

For the first and only time in my whole life I watch my footsteps as I cross Old Bridge. Toe first, heel second.

Reach her summit, feel my body leaning through her railings. Look around.

See the whole town glisten as the sun rises.

See the water sparkle.

See the mountains.

All the colour. All the laughter. All the life returned.

I'm nineteen again, and I don't think I'm ready to go home just yet.

LEILA. Me neither.

EMINA. I mean… we could just stay up all night?

MILI. We have stayed up all night.

LEILA.…My mum's gonna kill me.

SASHA. Well if this is your last day on earth we might as well enjoy ourselves.

MILI. Shall we grab a coffee?

EMINA.... Yeah. I think I'd like that.

Heels clink off old stone.

LEILA. Oh my God, babe, how are you still wearing heels?

EMINA. 'Because we've got the rest of our lives to wear sensible shoes.'

I pull my head back through the railings.

Toe first, heel second, all the way down.

And as I walk along the riverbank towards my old home, I turn around to see her one more time. Smiling as I –

A blast of tank fire interrupts her. A lingering and deep reverberation that echoes endlessly between the mountains, shakes your soul.

The earth beneath me trembles, throws me to the ground. Ears are ringing, something must have hit me, check my body, not a scratch but I can't hear a thing. I pull myself back on my feet. Regain my balance –

Another shot is fired. Tectonic plates fissure and tear. A colossus has awoken, and you can hear its pain.

Breathe in.

Breathe out.

Rub the dust out of my eyes...

Look ahead.

Feel my soul grow cold.

The only word that can leave my mouth is no louder than a whisper...

'Please.'

Another blast.

'Please don't…'

And another.

But it's no use.

And another.

Everything…

And another.

Everything I'd seen so far…

And another.

I could believe.

…But not this.

The only thing I'd never thought was possible…

One.

Last.

Fatal.

Shot.

Old Bridge splinters, breaks, and collapses into the river with all her weight as four hundred years of pain reverberates through the mountains.

The ungodly sound of Eternity screaming as she tears herself from the earth.

Rock… and iron… and history collapse into the river beneath.

This once clear water now white with stone and shame, as a thousand first kisses are washed away forever.

She stands there watching as the tsunami settles.

Silence.

Eternal silence.

I have lived to be older than Old Bridge.

Have lived long enough to know that there is nothing left for me to see.

Not in this world, at least.

And as I look up towards the mountains, I feel the sunshine sparkle as it makes me glow. Makes me clear for all to see as I know now with perfect clarity that this is where I die.

A sniper fires a shot in the distance. A crack as it lands next to her.

She looks gently to her left.

I think of you... in here, with me... I think of every loss and hardship that you will never have to live through and it brings me peace. What kind of animal... what kind of monster would bring a child into *this*. A town named after a bridge with no bridges left, where everything and everyone you ever cared about gets stolen from you one by one. Ripped away from you, one after the other until you have *nothing*!

...Until you *are* nothing.

I couldn't do that to a child.

I couldn't do that to you...

I'd never forgive myself.

He fires another shot. It lands next to her.

She looks to her right... Then straight at him.

COME ON! You can do better than that! Listen to the wind, I tell him, please!

...Nothing.

He only wants to kill me if I want to live... To steal something I care about but there's nothing left. I look at him and wait for silence but it doesn't come... So I make it easy for him.

She falls to her knees in prayer.

Allaaaaaaahu Akbar!

Aoozu billahi mina ash shaytanir rajeem.
Bis-millaahir rahmaanir raheem.

She kneels forwards, touching her forehead on the floor.

And as I pray for the first time in my life, a thousand memories consume mind and fill me with shame. With every regret I never knew I had. Every time Mrs Hasanović invited me for dinner and I just said no. Every moment longer that I could've had with Leila if I wasn't running late. Every chance I had to grab Mili by the hand and run towards that life I'd always dreamt of, and a hundred thousand more.

She kneels forwards, touching her forehead on the floor.

The shame as I feel you here, smaller than the smallest little thing, knowing that you heard those words. Knowing that you'll hate me for even thinking them, but you don't…

I just feel you smiling…

Laughing as you say 'Hey… hello. I think God's busy, but maybe I can help? I know this world's not perfect, but I'd still like to see it for myself sometime. Only if that's no trouble though?'

Silence.

And as I wrap my arms around you even tighter, I can't help but think that…

That maybe…

…Maybe that didn't sound so bad after all.

I open my eyes, look around and everyone I'd ever loved is standing on this cliffside next to me. Watching me as I am filled with every kindness that the world has ever shown me. Makes me weightless, heals these cuts and wounds, as I feel myself rising to my feet.

And as the thought of meeting you one day now beams across my face… I give the man up on that mountain something he can take from me, and I know this time he won't miss.

But as it turns out… God wasn't busy after all.

SASHA (*off*). HEY! DICKHEAD! OVER HERE!

He whistles loudly.

EMINA.... and neither was Sasha.

SASHA (*off*). HEY LOOK AT ME!

EMINA. In all the years that we'd been friends... of all the stupid things that he had ever done... I'm pretty sure this one outdid them all.

SASHA (*off*). Mina, run! LOOK AT ME YOU FUCKING –

SASHA *empties the entire clip of his rifle.*

Enter SASHA.

He runs towards EMINA, *rifle in hand.*

Blackout a second before they make contact.

PART FOUR – Didn't We Almost Have It All

4.1

Apartment, 1994 and present.

Daylight illuminates their ruined home for the first time.
Furniture lays broken, graffiti and bullet holes line the walls.
Empty tins of food lie eaten and discarded.

The dust is so thick the morning sunbeams leave a trail from the
window. An almost ethereal glow.

Enter MINA. *She's seven months pregnant.*

She stands in the centre of the room, alone. Numb. She spots the
charred remains of the photo album, burnt in the corner along
with other non-valuables. She picks it up, flicking through the
pages for anything that might be salvageable. There's nothing.
No photographs, and no emotions left to cry for them.

Unsure of where to begin, she finds a broom and begins
sweeping; an almost futile endeavour against the scale of
damage around her.

EMINA *lights the stove, fills a copper džezva with water from*
the tap, and starts making coffee.

A knock at the door. Tentatively MINA *answer it.*

EMINA. Six months later and a package finally arrives.

> *She comes back with a small brown parcel. Opening it, she*
> *finds a copy of* Vogue *and a birthday card: anachronisms in*
> *this world of broken things.*

Three years late… and sent to a girl that didn't exist.

It's the day of the jump and the sun is shining for the first
time in years. 'Any news, Emina?' I turn around and Mrs
Hasanović is sat on her porch. Alone.

> MINA *stops suddenly. She turns around and stares at the*
> *gap in the floorboards where she hid the Polaroid. She walks*

*over, takes a pin out of her hair and slowly fishes the photo
out; staring at it with eyes wide.*

No, I tell her… No news. I take the only photo that I have of
him, of us, and I hold it up to her… 'Still looking.'

I ask her if she's going to the jump and she just laughs…
'No', she says, 'no I don't think I can.'

She asks me why I'm going alone and I tell her Sasha can't
face it either. Well, she says… 'No climbing around like you
used to, you're seven months pregnant.' I just laugh. Tell her
I won't make any promises.

A moment as she smiles.

And as I wave her goodbye she calls out after me again. Her
voice different this time. I know exactly what she's gonna
say but I just raise my hand and –

'I know… I know… I just need something to bury, that's all.'

As I walk through Mostar's empty streets I hear that distant
clamour of a far-off crowd and I'm almost running.

A cheering crowd can be heard in the distance.

I weave my way through market stalls piled high with
vegetables, fresh fruit and coffee once again. Walk down
towards the beach as quickly as I can where –

The noise envelopes her.

If you'd told me a year ago there were this many people still
alive in Mostar, I wouldn't have believed you, and yet here
they all are.

I make my way through the crowd and find that perfect spot
where Old Bridge blocks the sun.

…Only now there's no shade.

She takes a big breath in.

I turn to the person in front of me. Tap them on the shoulder
and show them the photo. 'I'm really sorry to bother you, I'm
looking for a friend of mine. I don't suppose you've seen him?'

She can barely hear me over the crowd. I point to him but she just shakes her head, says I'm sorry.

A moment to breathe in, deeply.

I find the next willing face. He takes the photo. Asks me when I saw him last.

November. Our flat got raided, but there were no bodies.

He tries. He really tries. Like all of them do. But he shakes his head.

And as I stop to look around, I realise that I'm not alone... everywhere around me is another hopeful face. Hundreds of them. Young and old. Each one holding a photo in their hands. But before any of us can tap another shoulder...

The waterfront goes wild as twelve boys take centre-stage. A sea of faces turn towards that clear blue sky as one of them steps forward. Curls his feet over the crumbling rock where Old Bridge once began. He raises up his arms in Lasta. Waiting carefully for that perfect moment... And not a second sooner than when he's ready... he leans forward, flicks his toes and flies.

A flawless jump from a bridge that wasn't there.

'Mina!... Minaaaa!'

I turn around and see Sasha in the distance, searching through the cheering crowd as the judges raise their cards; I shout back. Wave to him until he sees me. Watch him as he pushes his way through. Breathless and panting.

Silence.

'They found him, Mina...

They found him.'

Her coffee is ready. She turns off the stove and pours herself a cup.

4.2

Apartment, present.

MINA *fades as her older self is left alone.*

EMINA. We're in a car, driving quickly. Neither of us is saying a word.

A field hospital a few miles south of Mostar; that's where they found him. Washed ashore, unconscious, no papers. Just the clothes he was wearing.

Three soldiers pulled him from the river. Managed to resuscitate him and brought him in. The only chance the doctors had was to put him in a coma and that's where he stayed for months.

After the fighting stopped, Sasha would drive to every hospital in town. Every hospital near town. Every mass grave whenever they found one. Each gathering crowd now a familiar set of faces, all waiting patiently for that day's list of names. Pinned to a noticeboard out front and read aloud by whichever hopeful face was feeling brave.

Every single day for six months, searching for answers with nothing but disappointment... until finally, one day, he finds the name he's looking for.

A blue and white flag flies high above a canvas city. I run up to the receptionist, start talking to him at a hundred miles an hour but he just shakes his head. Points towards an endless sea of chairs where row after row of lifeless faces wait in silence; each one clutching a photo of their own. We take a seat.

Three hours...

Three hours that were longer than the six months he was missing.

A doctor walks in. Reads my name out twice before I realise that it's mine she's trying to say. Sasha runs over, asks me to translate and I do...

In short it was a miracle that he was alive at all... but he wouldn't be getting better.

In the best English I could manage, I ask her:

'Can I see him, please?'

The room disappears.

4.3

UN Field Hospital, Jasenica, 1994.

An ECG machine beeps steadily as MILI *sleeps on a hospital bed, a ventilator mask across his mouth and nose.*

Enter MINA. *She and* EMINA *slowly become one, mirroring one another as their timelines finally merge.*

They see him.

Approach him slowly.

Feel him.

They hold his hand in disbelief that it's really him.

EMINA....He was so thin.

So peaceful lying there. I didn't want to wake him, but as I brushed the hair out of his eyes...

MILI*'s eyes open.*

MILI....Hello, my love.

MINA *runs her fingers through his hair. Kisses him on the forehead.*

MINA....Found you.

He shakes his head, smiling.

MILI. No... I found *you.*

They climb up onto the bed. Sit next to him.

Where's Sasha?

MINA. He's just outside.

MILI. ...and Leila?

MINA. ...Yeah. Leila too.

MINA curls up into him. Takes his arm and wraps it around her like a blanket as EMINA sits by his feet.

MILI. Oh... (*Re:* MINA*'s bump*.) who's this?

MINA. This? This is our little girl.

He pulls MINA into him, tight against his chest.

MILI. Does she have a name?

MINA. She does yeah.

MILI. ...What is it?

EMINA. It's *Millie*, I tell him... I'm gonna call her Millie.

MILI. Millie? But that's a boy's name.

EMINA. Not in England. In England it's a girl's name.

Silence.

MINA. Say something, hun.

MILI. ...If I told you everything I ever wanted was right here in front of me, would you still think I was boring?

MINA. You haven't bored me for a single second. Not from the moment I met you.

MILI. ...I can hear Sasha being sick outside.

MINA. Oh shush.

They laugh.

What happened to you, Mili? Where did you go?

EMINA disappears as the two of them are alone.

Time stands still.

MILI *removes his ventilator. Pulls his bedsheet off and sits upright.*

He's wearing the swimming trunks from the first day they met.

MILI....I ran, Mina.

Ran as fast as I could but they chased me... I knew if I caught up with you they would get us both, so I had to lose them, took the longest route I could. But when I got to Old Bridge... she wasn't there any more, and I could hear them coming.

I didn't know what to do, Mina, I just stood there. Curled my toes over the edge and closed my eyes.

I thought of you...

I thought of this one...

Waterfront, 1988.

They take a seat on the riverfront.

And when I opened them again, it was the day after we first met. The day of the jump, and it's so sunny. Ten thousand pairs of eyes are watching me, cheering my name, but I'm only thinking about one of them and even though you're a mile away, I can see you watching me from those cliffs and all I can think is... I'm gonna spend the rest of my life with her.

I raise my arms to the side and they go quiet. I close my eyes again and listen to the wind just like you taught me; I wait for it and I keep waiting, and I'll wait for an eternity if I have to because I need to get this right... and then the wind stops, and I hear you whisper... 'Now.'

I lean forward... and I fly.

MINA....How did you do?

MILI. It was the most perfect Lasta anyone had ever seen. Not a splash...

I swim to the surface, wipe the water from my eyes and look up at the judges but they're gone. I turn to look at the crowd but they've disappeared as well... It's just you. Alone on the beach, in your white dress. That perfect spot where Old Bridge blocks the sun… I climb out of the water and walk up to you. You smile at me but you don't say a word. I ask you what you thought of my jump, and you know what you said to me?

MINA. What?

MILI. 'It was alright I guess… I wasn't really paying attention.'

She laughs.

She cries.

Hospital, 1994.

MILI *sits back on the bed and* MINA *joins him. He lies down and pulls the blanket over himself. He gives her a long, slow kiss on the forehead before putting the mask back on and closing his eyes.*

EMINA. I fell asleep between his shoulders. Days, weeks, I don't know how long for but it felt like a lifetime.

Every sleep we never got to have. Every sleep that was stolen from us, we had then.

I just held his hand, and…

Silence.

And that was it…

That was the last time I ever saw him.

EMINA *looks out of the window as if it were the call-to-prayer, but instead of the Adhan, we hear Whitney Houston sing 'Didn't We Almost Have It All'. As she does, the flat is cleansed; the bullet holes, the broken furniture, the bloodstains and the graffiti.*

All of it fades into memory, as MILI *and* MINA *disappear forever.*

PART FIVE – The Time of My Life

5.1

Stone Plateau, 2004.

SASHA (*thirty-five*) *sits alone, smoking.*

Enter EMINA, *wearing a headscarf.*

EMINA.…I thought you weren't coming?

> SASHA *shrugs.*

SASHA. I wasn't. I just… I dunno. Work let me go early, so…

> *He stubs a cigarette out on the ground and lights another.*

EMINA. How was your shift?

SASHA.…Every time a tourist asks me to put milk in their coffee I just smile and try not to gag.

EMINA. It's a job, right?

SASHA. Yeah, well, it's hardly veterinary science but it's something to do I guess.

> *She sits down next to him.*

…You look good.

EMINA. Thanks. You look like shit.

> *They both laugh. He takes a bottle of flammable liquid out of his bag and some beers for* EMINA.

SASHA. I bought you some beers. I wasn't sure what to bring you so –

> *He holds one out to her.*

EMINA. Oh… I –

SASHA. Shit, sorry! Sorry! I… I'm so… *stupid*!

> *He hits himself.*

EMINA. Hey! Hey, you're not stupid, it's fine.

He tries to settle but he's tense. Nervous next to her.

SASHA. Will He smite you down if I have one next to you?

EMINA. I wear this for me, Sasha… No one else.

He smiles. Opens the bottle and takes a large sip.

SASHA.…How's the little one?

EMINA. 'The little one' is almost ten years old so sooner or later you're gonna have to start using her name.

Nothing. Silence. EMINA *takes a big breath in.*

She's okay, thank you. Not great with fireworks so Mrs Hasanović has got her.

She misses you… we both do.

SASHA. Yeah, well… I miss me too.

Silence. He drinks. Puts his cigarette out and lights another.

EMINA. The ridges on the back of his hand protruded as he pulled each cigarette away from his mouth. Thirty-five. Skinny. Grey in the face. That spark that lit up any room he entered faded long ago.

We used to spend each day together. Sometimes talking, sometimes laughing. Sometimes just sipping our coffees in comfortable silence… But eventually those coffees became something stronger, and those comfortable silences became, well… silences.

SASHA. Mina, I…

Sometimes I…

EMINA.…Go on.

SASHA. It's like… it's like sometimes the words aren't there, you know? Like I can feel them right there in front of me, but when I… It's like I can't…

He tries. He really tries but he can't. She takes his hand.

EMINA. It took me ten years to find mine… And I'm still looking for some of them. But they'll come, one day… and when they do they'll set you free, I promise.

Fireworks light up their faces as they look up in wonder.

Old Bridge sparkles in the sunshine as celebrities and politicians pose for photographs. Journalists from every TV station. Speedboats up and down the river, fleets of helicopters. I mean Prince Charles was here, for God's sake. My auntie begged me to get a photo with him but you couldn't even get close. All the locals had to watch on TV screens except for a handful of lucky ballot winners. I didn't manage to win a ticket... But you don't grow up in a town like this without learning one or two little secrets.

And once speeches were given and ribbons were cut, the music didn't stop all night. The whole of Mostar flooded on to the waterfront, queuing in their thousands for a chance to say they crossed Old Bridge the day she was reborn.

Come on, Sash, let's go!

SASHA....She's too clean.

EMINA. I know... I know she is, but one day she won't be!

SASHA. Yeah, you're right... we just have to wait another four hundred years.

He stands up, goes to leave.

EMINA. Sasha!

He stops. Turns around. Tears streaming down his face.

SASHA. You go cross your bridge, Emina! I'm going home.

EMINA. Come with me. Please! It'll be fun. Just like we –

SASHA. You don't get it, do you? I don't want a new bridge!

SASHA *starts crying uncontrollably.*

I miss them, Mina! I miss them with everything I am and I can't make it stop!

She runs to him and hugs him with all her strength.

EMINA....I didn't know it then, but this would be one of the last times I ever saw him.

In a couple of months this quiet little town would return to... well, exactly that. One by one the politicians and celebrities would all leave, and all those fancy hotels with their fancy coffee shops… well, they wouldn't need us any more.

Silence.

It would be ten days before anyone found him. An old friend from the army would pass by his house, go to knock on his front door and find it open. He'd look inside, call out his name, and catch just a glimpse of him through a gap in the bathroom door. Sat in the bathtub so he wouldn't make a mess. An empty box of whatever the doctors had given him, a bottle of the best whiskey he could afford and a shaving razor.

A small note on the kitchen counter, that's all he'd leave behind. Written on the back of a receipt with a hand so unsteady I could barely make it out:

'I'm sorry, Mina. Don't be angry with me. Please.'

Silence.

SASHA. I can't come with you… I can't do it. I want to, I just…

EMINA. What are you scared of, Sasha?

SASHA. I'm scared she'll be exactly the same!

EMINA. …No one's trying to bring back the past. No one… This is about the future and you have to look forward. You have to come with me. Please.

Silence.

SASHA. …What if it doesn't work?

EMINA. If it doesn't work then…

A moment.

I'll always know you tried.

She offers him her hand. As he takes it he disappears. As does the waterfront, the spectators, the fireworks. Everything.

Just EMINA, *alone.*

Apartment, present.

Three hours. That's how long we queued. Three hours of smiling ear to ear as I felt my body trembling. And every time I smiled at Sasha, he'd smile right back at me.

A hundred people packed around us so tightly I couldn't even see the ground.

But when that first step came... we didn't have to look. Like running up the steps of your own home.

Toe first.

Heel second.

All.

The way.

To the top.

Adhan. Church bells.

Epilogue – Show Me Heaven

Apartment, 1989.

Lights come up and everything is how it should have been forever:

SASHA, LEILA, MILI *and* MINA, *all dressed for the decade.*

'(I've Had) The Time of My Life' plays on the cassette player. SASHA *plays along, wearing his 'Choose Life' T-shirt.* LEILA *is curled up into him.*

MILI *and* MINA *stand facing each other, ready to start a dance routine that they've clearly been practising.*

As Bill and Jennifer sing, they start to rumba. LEILA *laughing and cringing. A misstep,* MILI *steps forward at the wrong time and knocks into* MINA.

MINA. Mili!

She walks over to the cassette player, rewinds the cassette and presses play.

SASHA *starts playing again.*

Properly this time, okay!

She counts them in and they do the routine as practised; pretty much MINA *dancing around him.*

The song approaches the chorus. She signals to him to try the lift.

MILI. No no no! Mina… Mina!

She runs up and jumps into him. He catches her against his chest.

The momentum knocks him backwards, and they land on the sofa.

Laughter from everyone.

LEILA. Mina, take a photo!

She picks up the camera and holds it out to take a selfie.

SASHA. Mili, can you move your gigantic head!

MILI. I can't, mate, your nose is in the way.

LEILA. Shush, you two!

MINA. Okay, come here a little, yep, okay, hold it...

Is everyone happy?

ALL. Yes!

As the camera flashes, blackout.

The last notes of the guitar fade into memory.

Silence.

The End.

A Nick Hern Book

Old Bridge first published in Great Britain in 2021 as a paperback original by Nick Hern Books Limited, The Glasshouse, 49a Goldhawk Road, London W12 8QP, in association with Papatango Theatre Company

Old Bridge copyright © 2021 Igor Memic

Igor Memic has asserted his right to be identified as the author of this work

Cover image by Dženis Hasanica

Designed and typeset by Nick Hern Books, London
Printed in Great Britain by Mimeo Ltd, Huntingdon, Cambridgeshire PE29 6XX

A CIP catalogue record for this book is available from the British Library

ISBN   978 1 84842 975 8